TRANSACTIONS

OF THE

AMERICAN PHILOSOPHICAL SOCIETY

HELD AT PHILADELPHIA
FOR PROMOTING USEFUL KNOWLEDGE

NEW SERIES—VOLUME 63, PART 2
1973

THEODORE ROOSEVELT AND HIS ENGLISH CORRESPONDENTS: A SPECIAL RELATIONSHIP OF FRIENDS

DAVID H. BURTON

Department of History, St. Joseph's College, Philadelphia

THE AMERICAN PHILOSOPHICAL SOCIETY
INDEPENDENCE SQUARE
PHILADELPHIA

MARCH, 1973

For
My Mother and My Brother
And
The Memory of My Father

Copyright © 1973 by The American Philosophical Society
Library of Congress Catalog
Card Number 73–75473
International Standard Book Number 0–87169–632–0

PREFACE

Lord Charnwood in the dedication of his biography of Theodore Roosevelt wrote of the man:

He was emphatically a plain American, which was why he was so much liked here in England, and nothing could have ever Anglicized him in the least. But he desired passionately the growth of understanding and of ready sympathy between the American people and the peoples of the British Empire, seeing that they are both trustees of a common heritage, and are so placed in the world that their concord can greatly further, their discord greatly hinder, the welfare of mankind.

Theodore Roosevelt would have honored this tribute, and his English friends would have esteemed it a true and honest appraisal. That historians and other readers concerned with the Anglo-American "special relationship" may come to some fuller awareness of its sources in its formative years, and more particularly, of the contributions of Roosevelt and certain of his English friends to the conception and building of the *de facto* alliance of the English-speaking peoples, I have written the pages that follow.

Many persons, both in England and America, have aided me in this understanding. Lady Arthur allowed me an unrestricted use of the papers of her late father, Sir Cecil Spring Rice; she is the ideal proprietress of family letters, at once generous, understanding, and alert to the meaning of history. Rose Hardcastle, executrix of the estate of the late Lady Lee, at great inconvenience to herself and to her husband, William Hardcastle, made the Lord Lee papers available. Amabel Williams-Ellis, the daughter of St. Loe Strachey, kindly has permitted me to quote from her father's letters, while at the offices of the *Spectator*, C. A. Seaton provided me access to the Strachey-Roosevelt letters and shared his quarters to make my task easier. I am grateful also to D. S. Porter, Department of Western Manuscripts, Bodleian Library, for placing the Bryce Papers Relating to the United States at my disposal. Alec Campbell of the University of Birmingham helped to light up obscure passageways of English history for me. A. Taylor Milne, formerly Secretary and Librarian, Institute of Historical Research, London University, was unfailing in his kindnesses. The staffs of the Historical Manuscripts Commission, Institute of Historical Research, Bodleian Library, and London University Library rendered real service. American friends and colleagues have been of great help as well. By her reminiscences, Alice Roosevelt Longworth imparted an ineffable freshness to TR's friendships with Spring Rice, Lee and the other correspondents. The late John B. Hughes aided me in an inimitable fashion, and I want to mention others as well, including Clarence C. Walton, William H. Harbaugh, Terrence Toland, S. J., the late Leslie J. Woods, William R. Forbes, and the late B. Hubert Cooper. My debt to the staff of the Manuscripts Division of the Library of Congress is worth special note.

I am pleased to thank the American Philosophical Society (Penrose Fund), St. Joseph's College (Faculty Research Fund) and the English-Speaking Union of the United States (Philadelphia Branch) for making monies available at critical junctures. Material reprinted from Elting E. Morison, Editor, *The Letters of Theodore Roosevelt* (8 v., Cambridge, Mass., 1951–1954) has been included with the permission of Harvard University Press and the President and Fellows of Harvard College, which permission is gratefully acknowledged.

In many ways and at many times my wife, Gerri, and my daughters, Antoinette, Monica, and Victoria, greatly aided me by their supply of inspiration and distraction—a happy mixture. The shortcomings of this study are my own entirely. And, after all, is the Anglo-American special relationship too elusive for the hour glass of mere analysis? The letters of Theodore Roosevelt and his English correspondents, as they fall into time and place, may persuade otherwise.

D. H. B.

3

THEODORE ROOSEVELT AND HIS ENGLISH CORRESPONDENTS: A SPECIAL RELATIONSHIP OF FRIENDS

David H. Burton

CONTENTS

INTRODUCTION

In an era when public men continued to look upon letter-writing as a means of setting forth ideas, developing thought, and justifying actions, Theodore Roosevelt earned a wide reputation as one of the great correspondents of the day. His letters ran to many thousands and though frequently he wrote with a consciousness of history, his correspondence betrayed the candor and the assertiveness, the honesty and the self-righteousness that characterized him as a public man. Among his most active correspondents were several well-known Englishmen, Cecil Spring Rice, Arthur Hamilton Lee, James Bryce, St. Loe Strachey, and George Otto Trevelyan. More as a result of letters than from the immediacy of their company Roosevelt came to know and to esteem these men as friends. Their exchange of thoughts through letters in each instance extended over a period of years and ranged over a wide list of topics of common concern. On the whole the letters reveal agreement and conflict, deep friendship and occasional distemper, with family notes interspersed among the larger issues in which all the correspondents were vitally involved. To read these letters is to share in an intimate fashion the growth of lifelong friendships and to witness from a privileged vantage point the rise of the Anglo-American rapprochement. From the early personal letters between Spring Rice and Roosevelt to the long, serious policy discussions of the 1914–1918 period the correspondence intertwines individual lives with great events, demonstrating the influence of men on the world in which they live. The letters tell persuasively how the Anglo-American entente came about and why it endured to become a "special relationship."

Historians have given the Anglo-American rapprochement appropriate attention. The present study is an effort to enlarge understanding of the great event by viewing it as the result, in part at least, of certain intellectual convictions shared by public men in England and the United States. The letters of Roosevelt and his English friends speak the character of the Anglo-American mind in a singular way. In these letters the intellectual roots of the alliance are evident, and though the focus is individualized, it is nonetheless suggestive of the large attitudes entertained by leaders in each country whose policies encouraged and then fructified the rapprochement. The alliance arose out of mutual advantage for England and America and their deliberate if piecemeal reaction to fast-changing conditions. Lacking certain common principles, well appreciated and sincerely believed in by both Roosevelt and his several correspondents—men who were in their own ways barometers of official and public opinion in the United States and Great Britain—it seems doubtful that the alliance would have blossomed as handsomely as it did. Nor is it likely that the friendship would have endured the strain fresh events exerted on it, save for those same underlying commitments.

Theodore Roosevelt corresponded with a great many English people, from King Edward VII to Parliamentary back benchers. He wrote and received letters from Cromer and Kipling and Edward Grey. But with five individuals in particular he corresponded consistently and at times intensively so that their letters over a period of years acquired a coherent pattern of thought. Of the five whose letters constitute the basis of this inquiry, not all were Roosevelt's friends in the conventional sense. St. Loe Strachey has pointed out in his autobiography that TR and he were in such accord and their ideas so confidentially shared he was amazed to realize what a comparatively few number of days, even hours, they had passed in each other's company. This was also the case with Trevelyan and Roosevelt. Bryce's dealings with TR while much more consistent were often times official. Arthur Lee saw

Roosevelt regularly only in 1898 and 1899, before his return to England to pursue his own career. Thereafter Lee made several trips to the United States while TR was in the White House; after that they were together briefly in 1910 and again in 1914. Spring Rice and Roosevelt were friends in a more usual fashion and saw much of each other in the late 1880's and early 1890's. Because of the exigencies of World War I they enjoyed little of each other's company while Spring Rice was British ambassador in Washington. Largely these men had a special kind of friendship, a friendship of letters. George O. Trevelyan chose to put it this way: "My vocation was only to return the balls struck over the net by the hand of the master." To a degree this judgment might be made regarding all the correspondents, though clearly it attributes too much to Roosevelt and far too little to the capacities of his friends. In the phrase of Dr. Johnson, each man "fairly put his mind" to the other. As TR remarked to Spring Rice in 1897: "You happen to have a mind which is interested in precisely the same things which interest me, and which I believe are of more vital consequences than any other to the future of the race and of the world; so naturally I am delighted to hear from you and I always want to answer your letters at length." For St. Loe Strachey it was a matter of minds "jumping together" like horses taking obstacles with the same stride.

Any number of hurdles along the course of Anglo-American relations had to be taken before the *de facto* entente of the two English-speaking nations assumed a clear and definite outline. The Spanish-American War saw England desert the continental Powers to sympathize with the United States and its war aims. Controversy over the fortification of an American-built canal at Panama and dissension growing out of the Alaska boundary feud were both serious obstacles to Anglo-American friendship, overcome only by British acquiescence to United States insistence on settlements favorable to America. In contrast the Boer War, like the Russo-Japanese War, involving vital British interests demanded and received circumspect United States consideration of British sensitivity and advantage. The total effect of Anglo-American diplomatic give-and-take encouraged leaders in America and England to look forward to the time when they could agree that all future differences between them were to be settled by arbitration. That the proposal for arbitration contained in the 1911 Arbitration Treaty died aborning reminded one and all that national interest and national sovereignty were not things lightly cast aside. The lesson of World War I for Anglo-American friendship was much the same. Genuine sympathy and mutual regard between the two countries did not lessen the height of the hurdles emplaced by the war in 1914, but gave to the riders the requisite seat and hands and nerve to clear these fresh barriers to understanding. America's entry into the war in 1917 worked to confirm the governing principle of an entente that got its first statement in 1898. This principle can be simply rendered: a clash of two national interests can always be resolved so long as there is the will and willingness to seek it.

Theodore Roosevelt was not a universally popular figure in England during the years 1898–1919. It could hardly have been otherwise because of the hard line he took with the London government on certain critical issues. Some of his actions were readily interpretable as anti-British. His strictures regarding certain English newspapermen, like Maurice Low, were pungent evidence of this; he once exclaimed that Low was a "circumcised skunk." More importantly, British officialdom, from the prime minister down, entertained a mixture of distrust and distemper toward the strongly nationalistic policies of the United States during Roosevelt's presidency when they were carried out at the expense of the British Empire. Even after the London government had acquiesced to American world pretension and accordingly had reformulated its policies, and Anglo-American accord was on the lips of many, among Foreign Office professionals America's friendship appeared little more than a tiresome necessity. Roosevelt overcame both public doubts and official reservations in part because his diplomacy, largely viewed, was consonant with Britain's advantage and in part because a host of friends in England made the man in the street there aware of this.

In using the letters I have been guided by several considerations. Whenever letters of significance are published here for the first time I have quoted them fully because of the requirements of the present study and as a service to other interested parties. Many of the longer extracts I have set off from the text, except where I felt the content could be accommodated to the flow of the narration. A few letters I have consigned to footnotes when they contained material of relevance the gist of which was discussed in another connection. Reluctantly, many letters of general value are not contained here because their content falls outside the scope of the present work. By and large I have followed a topical arrangement in chapters one and two and a chronological pattern in chapters three and four, with somewhat greater attention shown the correspondence after 1914.

I. FRIENDS

Of all Theodore Roosevelt's English friends none was more dear to him than Cecil Spring Rice. The two met in 1886 on a trans-Atlantic crossing to England, at a time when their careers, which were to be surprisingly important parts of the larger friendship of their two countries, promised much. They were diverse characters: Roosevelt, the man of action, Spring Rice of a poetic, reflective disposition. Born a year apart, scarcely twelve months separated them in death. The introspective strain in TR's make-up was resilient enough to provide a viable response to his friend's poetic instinct. Spring Rice's own career that included tenure at diplomatic stations halfway round the world only whetted Roosevelt's curiosity about Berlin or Constantinople, Persia or Russia, for he wrote numerous letters rich in description of the things he witnessed, the people he met, and the historical forces that appeared to be at work, shaping, and at times threatening, the future of their peoples. In composing these dispatches Spring Rice showed how well he knew his American friend. From Berlin in July of 1896 he offered his impressions of the German military.

As a matter of fact soldiers one sees (and regiments go by every day) look splendidly—marching well, and looking proud and pleased. It must in the long run be good for a nation to take all the young men of a certain age for two years—clean them, feed them, drill them, teach them obedience and patriotism, and train their bodies. The officers are rather different to ours. A prince (and there are numbers of them) has to do exactly as the others do—that is, get up at five and work his men and his own training till four in the afternoon.[1]

Here was the diplomat on station, in his own way a man of action, supplying Roosevelt with a vicarious sense of soldiering. Only partly did Spring Rice recount such an impression because of TR's martial enthusiasms. Equally important, and equally valuable for seeing through to the essence of their friendship, was the possible implication for the Anglo-American peoples of the rise of the new Germany. In this same letter Spring Rice introduced another note that underscored his profound uneasiness about the future: the specter of Russia. "I think the Russians have got the Chinese now whenever they like," he told Roosevelt; "when they command and drill the Northern Chinese they will be a pretty big power—such a power as the world has never seen."[2] Often in years to come Roosevelt and Spring Rice pondered together the ambitions of Germany, the destiny of Russia, and the uncertainties in the Orient, and in what best ways Great Britain and the United States, or the two nations working as one, must act to protect themselves. For both of them it amounted to a combination of thought and action and though the mixture differed for each man, they enjoyed a common ground.

Roosevelt's reply to this early letter of Spring Rice disclosed further dimensions of their mutual fondness. He told how he and his wife had eagerly read and re-read his letter and had repeated parts of it for their children. "As you know," Roosevelt wrote, "we are not fond of many people, and we are very fond of you, and if you don't come back to America for ten years, yet whenever you do, you will find us just as anxious to see you as we always were in the old days in Wash-

ington."[3] Spring Rice was witty, urbane, keen on the children, and in what were still bachelor days for him, the Roosevelt home-life was surely attractive. During these years he came to value the friendship of Edith Carow Roosevelt. "Mrs. Roosevelt always refers to your last visit as one during which she got really to be more and more glad that you were in the house, so that she felt as if one of the family had gone when you left," TR confided to Spring Rice on one occasion.[4] Few of the people Roosevelt enjoyed earned the affection of his wife so that Spring Rice was all the more welcomed in the household. As the years went by he wrote Edith Carow on frequent occasions, especially when Roosevelt was president. He had her confidence and felt that, at times, it was more discreet to express himself fully on some delicate pending issue to her, assured that the president would receive his message. Writing to Mrs. Roosevelt from St. Petersburg in December, 1903, he asked coyly: "Would you like a disquisition on politics here?" Whereupon several paragraphs concerned with taxation, the weaknesses of the Russian government, conformity in Russian society followed. Then he added: "All this is rather dull for you, but it is amusing to me, however dull it is to hear about." The president, in turn, would know his thoughts.[5]

Spring Rice was not, however, merely exploiting his acceptance by Edith Carow Roosevelt. As often their letters dealt with family and the children, with tales of happy adventure or nostalgic comments on past pleasures, and because Spring Rice was a poet, an occasional romantic description of Santa Sophia or the Persian countryside.[6] Perhaps he found it easier to write his deeper feelings about TR to his friend's wife than directly to him. "The more I think of Theodore, and I think of him constantly—I believe every day of my life—I think I know him as a pure, high, noble and devoted character as it is possible to find in our present world."[7] These lines to Edith Roosevelt leave small doubt of his affection. Occasionally sentiment did break through as when he wrote at length to TR himself congratulating him on his election as New York governor. The letter concluded: "the great thing is to retain the power of being fond of people and that I have done, and most especially of you."[8] Mrs. Roosevelt's letters reciprocated Spring Rice's feelings. "I wish you knew how often we speak of you and how much we want to see you," she wrote him while he was in Persia.

---

[3] Roosevelt to Spring Rice, Aug. 5, 1896, *Roosevelt Letters* 1: p. 553.

[4] *Ibid.*

[5] Spring Rice to Edith Carow Roosevelt, Dec. 9, 1903, Gwynn, 1929: 1: pp. 372–374.

[6] For example, Edith Carow Roosevelt to Spring Rice, Dec. 15, 1897, *ibid.* 1: p. 326; Spring Rice to Edith Carow Roosevelt, Dec. 22, 1898, *ibid.* 1: p. 271.

[7] Spring Rice to Edith Carow Roosevelt, July, 1898, Spring Rice Papers.

[8] Spring Rice to Roosevelt, Nov. 1898, *ibid.*

---

[1] Spring Rice to Roosevelt, July 18, 1896, Gwynn, 1929: 1: p. 208.

[2] *Ibid.*

Do you remember that year that little Ted was so ill, and you used to ride up to the steps of the tiny Jefferson Place house with your pockets full of wild flowers for him? I can see him and Alice now making a baby garden by sticking the flowers in the seat of the cain chair. . . . Please come back before we are all too staid and middle aged.[9]

Though much in the official careers of Roosevelt and Spring Rice related to the large affairs of state, the two watched with satisfaction the personal successes visited upon the other. TR's was the more meteoric rise to power, Spring Rice's the more conformable to pattern: steady, patient, and at the last impressive in its achievement. It was also predictable. Born in London in 1859 the second son of the Hon. Charles Spring Rice, he was educated at Eton and Balliol. In 1882 he entered the Foreign Office where his father had once served. After gaining valuable experience as private secretary to Lord Granville and as a précis-writer for Lord Roseberry, he was posted to the British legation in Washington in 1886. Meeting Roosevelt quite accidentally on shipboard in November of that year they quickly became such good friends that Spring Rice stood as best man at the Roosevelt-Carow wedding which took place at St. George's, Hanover Square, in December. With his usual thoughtfulness he made the stay in London a pleasurable one for his new friends.

By the mid-1890's the careers of both men had taken steps forward and each was eager for the promotion of the other. With an eye to the outcome of the presidential election of 1896 Spring Rice wrote from Berlin at a time when TR was New York City police commissioner: "I hope . . . that you will get something extremely nice in Washington if you wish to go back, and if not, something that will give you a change in New York." [10] And there was both congratulation and admiration as Roosevelt wrote his friend when he was posted to Berlin.[11] Meanwhile Roosevelt's march on history took on a quickened cadence. "I am perfectly delighted that you are Governor," Spring Rice enthused in November, 1898. "I wish you were a Senator, but that is to come." [12] When TR was elected president in his own right—the summit of his political success—his English friend "chortled with delight" and wished he could be in Washington to see him. "This is the very best news I have had for ages. . . . It is simply grand," his letter read.[13]

This same personal quality motivated the president to prefer Spring Rice as British ambassador to the United States when the London government undertook to name

a successor to Sir Julian Paunceforte in 1903. "Great Heavens, how I wish you were Ambassador here!" he wrote quite frankly to Spring Rice. "There are fifty matters that came up that I would like to discuss with you, notably about affairs in the Far East, and you could be of great service to your own country as well as this country." [14] Spring Rice in fact came to Washington in 1905 with the approval of Lord Lansdowne at a time when the president was attempting to make arrangements for peace talks between Russia and Japan. At that time the British government was unwilling to exert pressure on her Japanese ally so that it made little difference if the president and the special emissary were old friends. In fact, as the letters of Roosevelt and his English correspondents reflect relations between the United States and Great Britain, friendship of a personal sort generally did not shape policy but greatly facilitated the formulation and execution of policies which appeared to be mutually attractive. But where, in the judgment of either Roosevelt or his friends, the national interests of the two countries were opposed then at best the friendships provided the means for a renewed effort at a solution acceptable to each side.

Spring Rice became ambassador to the United States in 1913, having served in the British legations in Persia and Sweden in the intervening years. Considered too inexperienced for the Washington assignment in the early years of the century, he served in Washington down to 1918, the critical period for testing and proving the Anglo-American rapprochement. From Stockholm, Spring Rice expressed his inner satisfaction at the prospect of being once more in America, and especially of reviving his association with the Roosevelts. With mock-cynicism he promised to abuse TR "as much as you like in public if you stand in need of such assistance. The condition being that Mrs. Roosevelt is kind to my wife." [15] It was to be like the good old days and his feelings were fully shared. "Three cheers!" exclaimed Roosevelt to his friend on learning of the appointment. "But now I feel horribly at not being President." [16] At about the same time TR wrote to Arthur Lee: "I am immensely pleased that Spring Rice is coming here. I hope it will make him brace up and remove that 'distressing resemblance to a sad shrunken Bulgarian king' which you say his beard has given him." [17] The career of each man had reached fruition, though the arc of success did not intersect at apogee. The stress of the Great War, and the diversity of national interest between America and England brought on by the conflict, troubled relations between the two friends as between the two nations. Yet there was something deeper between them, the shared experience of happier times which not even the large concerns of state could

[9] Edith Carow Roosevelt to Spring Rice, Dec. 15, 1899, Gwynn, 1929: 1: p. 326; see also, to Spring Rice, March 25, 1900, Spring Rice Papers.

[10] Spring Rice to Roosevelt, July 18, 1896, ibid.

[11] Roosevelt to Spring Rice, Aug. 5, 1896, Roosevelt Letters 1: p. 555.

[12] Spring Rice to Roosevelt, Nov. 15, 1898, Gwynn, 1929: 1: p. 268.

[13] Spring Rice to Roosevelt, Nov. 9, 1904, ibid., p. 435; to Roosevelt, Dec. 7, 1904, ibid., p. 438.

[14] Roosevelt to Spring Rice, Nov. 9, 1904, ibid., p. 434.

[15] Spring Rice to Roosevelt, Dec. 11, 1912, Roosevelt Papers.

[16] Roosevelt to Spring Rice, Nov. 12, 1912, Roosevelt Letters 7: p. 638.

[17] Roosevelt to Lee, Dec. 31, 1912, ibid. 7: p. 683.

efface. The old affection was poignantly evident as Spring Rice wrote Roosevelt in 1915 about the death of Henry Cabot Lodge's wife.

Mrs. Lodge's death is the end of many things—more than I can say. It is a blow quite irreparable to my wife and me. . . . What times we had in Washington and what things we can remember! What immense changes, not only in the friends who used to meet and walk together but in the background. At any rate, we are the masters of our own souls.[18]

The demands of the war and the passing of time had made the old days irrecoverable, and the meaning of them more dear.

"You must always remember that the President is about six," Spring Rice had occasion to write Valentine Chirol. The remark is often quoted to expose the childishness of Roosevelt or the cynicism of its author. But can it tell something of the Roosevelt-Spring Rice relationship? Spring Rice made the comment to Chirol to whom he had given a warm letter of introduction to the president. Theirs was a disappointing meeting, despite the ardor of Spring Rice's favor, so that in writing Chirol as he did he was attempting to soothe the latter's frustration at not winning Roosevelt's acceptance. No doubt his wit exceeded his good judgment in the matter. Spring Rice himself must have felt let down that his two friends, Roosevelt and Chirol, could not have been friends also. A similar feeling of disappointment on the part of Roosevelt and his English friends became visible when some practical issue arose between their two countries. American and Englishman alike preferred a settlement of such disputes along lines of their own national interest. In like fashion Spring Rice found in Roosevelt and Chirol people of whom he was genuinely fond. But he could not allow his liking for one to blind him to the other. This was the strength of the Anglo-American special relationship as well: national advantage ought to be pursued, even at the expense of the other partner. That diverse national interests did not finally divide England and America but curiously added strength to their entente was due to the common Anglo-American commitments, which TR and his English correspondents typified. As for the two men, disagreements and quirks of character aside: Roosevelt's frenetic ways and Spring Rice's relentless wit, they remained brothers to the last.

Of the tributes Theodore Roosevelt might have offered to Arthur Hamilton Lee, the proudest was that he had been with TR in Cuba. A captain at the time, Lee had been seconded from the Royal Canadian Military College to serve as the British military attaché with the American army operating in the Caribbean in 1898. The common experience as a Rough Rider commenced and cemented a friendship that was as firm in 1918 as it had been promising in '98. The friendship ripened quickly. "You can treat him [Lee] as you can trust me," Roosevelt confided to Elihu Root, "and in speaking to him you are not only speaking to an officer and gentleman representing the country to which we are most closely bound but also a thorough expert in his business and as staunch a friend as America has." [19] Less than a year before his death, TR wrote Lee: "My dear Arthur, I have literally never had a friend who combined as you do absolute loyalty with complete understanding and sympathy. And you combine a further and even rarer combination—insight and common sense with courage and humor." [20]

Their early correspondence was taken up with military matters. Roosevelt discussed with Lee some of the difficulties of the Cuban campaign, commenting unsparingly on the United States Army: "the utter lack of administrative skill shown before Santiago as well as the fact that there was literally no generalship whatsoever." [21] The shortcomings of the American army were pretty well known throughout European military circles, Lee told the ex-Colonel of Rough Riders, writing what he termed "delicious" anecdotes to underscore his point.[22] As the occasion and need of concern with military affairs passed the mutual interests of the two friends broadened to historical and political views and to personal matters. In 1899 Lee married an American heiress, Ruth Ellen Moore, as was the becoming style of many English gentlemen of the day.[23] In September of 1899 he told Roosevelt of his engagement: "the biggest thing that can come into any decent man's life has just come into mine, and I am engaged to be married to the sweetest and best girl in America." [24] The marriage heightened Lee's devotion to Anglo-American friendship. When he returned to England to enter politics he became passionately pro-American. "One of the chief planks in my platform was 'Friendly with America'," he informed Roosevelt, "and you will be glad to hear that it was perhaps the most popular of all my planks—a fact which was no doubt largely due to the striking object lesson I was able to show in my

[18] Spring Rice to Roosevelt, Oct. 10, 1915, Gwynn, 1929: 1: p. 293; see also Roosevelt to Spring Rice, Feb. 18, 1916, *Roosevelt Letters* 8: p. 891; also to Spring Rice, July 6, 1913, *ibid.* 7: p. 737.

[19] Roosevelt to Root, Sept. 2, 1899, Roosevelt Papers.

[20] Roosevelt to Lee, April 12, 1918, Lee Papers.

[21] Roosevelt to Lee, Sept. 2, 1899, *ibid.*

[22] Lee to Roosevelt, March 14, 1899, Roosevelt Papers. For highlights and sidelights of Lee's experience as a British observer with American forces in the Spanish-American War see E. Ranson, "British Military and Naval Observers in the Spanish-American War," *Jour. Amer. Studies* 3 (1969): pp. 33–56.

[23] Lee himself commented to this effect. "My wife is enjoying her new life immensely and is the greatest possible help to me in my work," he told TR. "Indeed it is the first essential to success over here now to have an American wife, and the latest music-hall joke describes English society as being controlled by 'Duchesses and other American ladies.' " Lee to Roosevelt, Nov. 22, 1903, Roosevelt Papers.

[24] Lee to Roosevelt, Sept. 24, 1899, *ibid.*

American wife." [25] The reply sounded much the same note, TR pointing out that in his collection of essays published in 1900 under the title *The Strenuous Life,* "you will see that there was no allusion to England that was not friendly." [26]

Having entered Parliament in 1900, Lee spoke candidly and intimately to Roosevelt of his reasons motivating the career he hoped to make for himself. [27] He represented a safe conservative district, Fareham, in Hampshire, and in 1903 joined the Balfour government as the cabinet office charged with the responsibility for naval preparedness; he remained in Parliament until World War I. Throughout these years Lee was on the friendliest terms with TR, and visited Washington several times while Roosevelt was president. He played host to Roosevelt during part of his 1910 stay in England and again in 1914. When war broke that year Lee once more entered military service. He was immediately seconded to France with the British Expeditionary Force where he was on the staff of General Sir John French. Twice mentioned in dispatches, Roosevelt's admiration for him "at the front" was supreme. He wrote Lee's wife to praise his soldierly qualities, recalling their days together in Cuba and lamenting that he had to be content to view the war from the sidelines. [28]

In the course of their relationship Lee displayed toward Roosevelt an unstinted admiration, combined with an instinctive feeling that his friend was destined for great things. Shortly after he received the vice-presidential nomination, Lee wrote with typical intent: "I hardly know what to say." Nature, he thought, had not intended TR to be a vice-president; he was "peculiarly unfitted to languish in the role of 'second-fiddle.'" "When the rivers are thrown violently out of their courses in this way, Providence must have a purpose in view that is not necessarily apparent on the surface." [29] McKinley's tragic death and Roosevelt's corresponding good fortune might be judged, therefore, as literally providential, even though Lee's comment may have been made in a less than totally serious vein. Certainly from that time on Lee was prepared to do the president's bidding. "I would come any place, any time, to talk with you," he insisted to Roosevelt, who saw in Lee a trusted and useful informant respecting the British political scene. [30]

Unlike the Spring Rice-Roosevelt friendship which was throughout its time one of equals, Arthur Lee, even with the passing of years, inclined to approach TR with a sense of awe. He could never quite bring himself to expect of his friend some favor or kindness without a special pleading though he was eager to be of the greatest service to Roosevelt. Arrangements for the ex-president's stay in England in 1910 particularly demonstrated this. Lee was fully determined that Roosevelt should be *his* guest while in London that year. England was the last leg of the famous Teddyssey which had begun on safari in British East Africa and included a number of European capitals before the grand finale of the grand tour in London. Lee's importunities of Roosevelt began before the latter had left the White House. He announced himself completely prepared to put himself at his friend's disposal.

It will not in the least matter when you arrive as we shall be ready for you any time next year, and your suite of rooms will be waiting for you and your party from now on. . . . We will in fact be your private hotel from which you can make side trips in visits wherever you like. . . . [31]

At about this time the Lees had come into possession of Chequers, the magnificent estate in Buckinghamshire subsequently given by them to the British government. Lee was anxious that Roosevelt should enjoy his hospitality there as well as at his town address. He even went so far as to arrange a proper English valet for the ex-president. [32] Roosevelt was forced to decline the total of Lee's generosity. For official reasons he first went to the American Embassy and learned that as arrangements had been made by the staff there it would be a week at least before he would be able to come to the Lees, punctuating his explanation with the rather unRooseveltian admission: "I had no choice." [33] Lee managed, nonetheless, to host a number of activities for his friend during the London sojourn, functioning as a kind of appointment secretary—"the rest of the programme I am keeping in as fluid a state as possible" —and in some measure influenced TR's itinerary. The English phase of Roosevelt's tour was a great success, in spite of the death at the time of King Edward VII, dramatizing the possibilities of Anglo-American accord. The presence of so distinguished an American in the funeral procession of the king for example, left the English people with an exceedingly favorable impression. The visit was also an important episode in the Roosevelt–Lee relationship. They were to see each other only once more when Roosevelt went back to England in 1914, in what Lee spoke of as "five days of delightful and stimulating memory." [34] By this time it was apparent that Roosevelt's health had been undermined by fever contracted in the Amazonian jungle. Lee warned the ex-president against a "swing-round the Middle West in August and 30 speeches a day from the tail of a Pullman car!" His ideal was that "you

[25] Lee to Roosevelt, Nov. 12, 1900, Roosevelt Papers.
[26] Roosevelt to Lee, Nov. 23, 1900, *Roosevelt Letters* 2: p. 1440.
[27] Lee to Roosevelt, July 19, 1900, Roosevelt Papers.
[28] Roosevelt to Ruth Ellen Moore Lee, Nov. 30, 1914; to Ruth Ellen Moore Lee, June 16, 1915, Lee Papers.
[29] Lee to Roosevelt, July 19, 1900, Roosevelt Papers.
[30] Lee to Roosevelt, Aug. 21, 1902, *ibid.*

[31] Lee to Roosevelt, March 1, 1909, *ibid.*
[32] Lee to Mr. Harper, May 9, 1910, *ibid.*
[33] Roosevelt to Lee, March 10, 1910, *Roosevelt Letters* 7: p. 54.
[34] Lee to Roosevelt, July 21, 1914, Roosevelt Papers.

will find yourself dwelling in all the odor of sanctity in a 'Wren' house, looking on Westminster Abbey. . . ." [35] Not a likely prospect, Roosevelt wrote thanking his host: "as soon as I got back here I was plunged into politics." [36] Shortly thereafter hostilities commenced in Europe; the war would bring Roosevelt and Lee closer together.

Despite Arthur Lee's inclination to defer to TR, especially in personal affairs, the health of their friendship derived in no small measure from Lee's willingness to make a temperate but unambiguous statement of the British point of view in a given controversy between the two English-speaking nations. Replying to a letter of March 18, 1901, wherein the vice-president had written forcefully of the American desire to fortify an Isthmian canal under direct United States control and of the justice of the American demands in the Alaskan boundary matter, Lee began by saying: "It is very good of you to write your views so frankly, and yet it is *only* by a frank interchange of views that our Peoples can hope to understand each other as they should." The mood of candor thus established, he spoke out against the American determination to build an American, as opposed to a neutral, canal.

Against this your people, may, of course, argue that their stand in this matter involved the national interest, to such an extent that they will sooner fight than give an inch. But is this *always* to be the answer of the U.S. when they can't get everything they want; and can you expect England always to give way simply because she regards the prospect of war with the U.S. as unthinkable?

Lee expressed similar views with similar emphasis respecting the Alaskan boundary dispute.

And now—as you raised the question in your letter—I must say a few words about the Alaska Boundary question, from our point of view. . . . It is here necessary to remember that in 1895–96 there was a boundary dispute between England and Venezuela. England thought she was right, whilst Venezuela was equally confident of her position. Whereupon the U.S. intervenes (with some aggressiveness!) and *insists* that England shall submit the whole dispute to arbitration. England agrees and the consequent proceedings vindicate her claims. Now, another boundary dispute arises with the U.S. as one of the parties concerned. England, mindful of the precedent of 1895–96, suggests arbitration. But the U.S. refuses—and says in effect, "Oh—no—we won't arbitrate about the boundary because Canada 'hasn't a leg to stand on.'" But . . . *if* the American case is so overwhelmingly sound why not accept arbitration, and so demonstrate the soundness of your claim before the whole world? [37]

Roosevelt valued such candor. "I was glad to hear from you," he replied; "it is not worth while writing at all if one can not write frankly." [38] Cool appraisal generally characterized the correspondence of Roosevelt

and his friends, a recognition that differences of opinion which were inevitable because of differing national interests, had to be faced squarely. The compelling consideration was to speak out freely on the issues, to learn the attitude of the other and to treat his position with respect, for in that way some workable resolution of the disagreement could be achieved. "I shall always cling hopefully to the belief that 'the better we get to know each other, the better we shall like each other,' " Lee once observed to Roosevelt. [39] Such hopes did not depend simply on the good will of Anglo-American statesmen or the friendliness of their peoples. Good will was present because of the kinship of the two peoples, a condition prompting mutual respect and trust on one hand and facilitating agreeable accommodation on another. Lee thought the common bond made England "always willing to go further in the way of concession and friendly service to the United States than to all other nations of the earth combined." "But it can not be all give and no take, and your people should remember that we are also very proud and very powerful." [40] Throughout their friendship this conviction of an ultimate basis for Anglo-American solidarity was an unwritten presupposition, to be acted upon positively by those individuals who accepted it as a working principle but who were at the same time aware of the limitations imposed by national interests.

Not all English leaders (nor American for that matter) recognized this working principle. Part of Arthur Lee's political purpose was to persuade those Englishmen of importance whom he met. He once told Roosevelt of giving Lord Lansdowne, Balfour, and other members of the government "some new lights on the American side of the case [of the canal];" and of a "useful talk with Lord Lansdowne, . . . and was I think able to correct in his mind a certain number of curious misapprehensions about your personality and your policy." [41] An awareness of England's "melancholy isolation" cast in far larger terms than "useful talks" with Arthur Lee did more to convince the British government of the need for a friendly America; yet Lee's personal diplomacy was at least a small force in the swelling tide of reassessment.

The personal element, it appeared to Lee, was critical. He urged upon Lansdowne the extreme desirability of appointing "none but the best men to any position on the staff of our Embassy in Washington" and explained to him "how detrimental it was to the interests of the two countries to place inferior or unsympathetic men in the most delicate position." [42] Noteworthy of the confidentiality with which he discussed such matters with President Roosevelt, Lee wrote deploring the practice and the likelihood of some one from the Diplomatic Service being named to the American ambassa-

[35] *Ibid.*

[36] Roosevelt to Lee, June 19, 1914, *Roosevelt Letters* 7: p. 769.

[37] Lee to Roosevelt, April 2, 1901, Roosevelt Papers. (Italics in original.)

[38] Roosevelt to Lee, April 24, 1901, *Roosevelt Letters* 3: p. 64.

[39] Lee to Roosevelt, April 2, 1901, Roosevelt Papers.

[40] *Ibid.*

[41] Lee to Roosevelt, Dec. 17, 1901, Roosevelt Papers.

[42] *Ibid.*

dorial post at a time when the advancing years of Lord Pauncefort made an opening probable. He went so far as to state his opposition to Sir Michael Herbert, whose appointment he deemed would be "unfortunate." [43] Herbert in fact won the position and as it developed, the president liked him. It can only be guessed that Herbert failed to become a White House intimate in the style of von Sternburg or Jusserand because of Lee's appraisal.

Not surprisingly the time came when Roosevelt preferred Lee as ambassador to Washington. On the day of McKinley's funeral the new president suggested to Lee that he send him an occasional, confidential report on the state of affairs and opinion in London for his information and use. [44] In 1906 Lee came for a White House visit and while there discussed a variety of topics from Chinese customs to Newfoundland fisheries. In some way therefore Lee was an unofficial ambassador. To make it official seemed both logical and suitable to the president. His choice of Lee was dictated by a desire to have someone "whom I know well and in whose judgment no less than his discretion I had complete confidence." Much of what was typical of the Roosevelt-Lee friendship, itself suggestive of the larger outlines of the Anglo-American rapprochement, was contained in the remainder of Roosevelt's argument in favor of Lee as ambassador to the United States.

You and I have campaigned together. You stand for your country's interest first, and I should not respect you if this were not the case. But so far as is compatible with first serving the interests of your country you have a genuine desire to do what is friendly to America. These are reasons why I asked you to come to see me and have made you my channel of communication. [45]

In 1906 the ambassadorial post fell vacant when Sir Mortimer Durand who had succeeded Herbert upon the latter's death, proved incapable of striding with the president, a critical qualification in TR's judgment for any British ambassador to Washington. Roosevelt's letter to Lee, dated November 5, 1906, left little doubt of his preference and, equally significant, spoke that very friendly, highly patriotic, supremely practical quality that characterized the Anglo-American entente.

I earnestly hope that if a change is made we shall have some man as nearly your stamp as possible. You are not one of those maudlin sentimentalists who will sacrifice the good of their country to an admirable but weak desire to be good to another country. I wouldn't request you if you were such a type because a representative of Great Britain who would not be true to Great Britain's interests would speedily lose weight in Great Britain, and I want to deal with some one who can influence Great Britain. But you know America. You can get on well with our people. You can speak to them and appear to advantage before them. You were an honorary member of my regiment and I can trust not merely your purpose but your judgment and

sagacity. If you were here you would visit Newfoundland and the Alaska seal fisheries yourself. . . . If as in the Jamaica business it was possible for England to do a good turn to America without hurt to herself I could call the matter to your attention. If I had you or some one exactly like you here, you would have known the entire Algeciras business just as Jusserand knew it. In China you would be kept in touch day by day with all that was going on, so that our two countries could act exactly on the same line. Surely all this is worthwhile. [46]

Roosevelt's disappointment at Lee's failure to get the post—his chances even with strong presidential support were remote—was somewhat softened by the appointment of James Bryce, another long-term correspondent and friend of the president.

Though Theodore Roosevelt welcomed the prospect of James Bryce as British ambassador, Bryce was never his intimate after the fashion of Spring Rice or Arthur Lee. There were good reasons for this. Bryce, twenty years Roosevelt's senior when they first became acquainted in the 1880's, had an already established reputation as a scholar, politician, and man of affairs. The advantage of years and in some ways of mind and experience which Bryce enjoyed showed itself even when TR was in his last months in the White House and Bryce was ambassador. Lord Curzon, chancellor of Oxford University, had invited the president to deliver the Romanes Lecture for 1910. Roosevelt looked forward to the occasion as a rare opportunity to discuss the method and meaning of history as well as providing some direction for future generations. "Biological Analogies in History," as the lecture was entitled, was TR's most ambitious foray into the intellectual world. He could have no better mentor than James Bryce, sometime Regius Professor of Law at Oxford, a student of many different lands and cultures, and a man who was by all accounts an intellectual of the first rank. Several times in the latter weeks of 1908 Bryce was at the White House, as the president himself put it, to "suffer the wholly unwarrantable torments which I design to inflict upon you by going over my Romanes lecture with you." [47] As a good mentor, Bryce looked at various drafts of the address, advising on two or three points the president was unsure of, and in effect giving it the imprimatur of a senior scholar. [48]

Despite the disparity of age Roosevelt and Bryce had much in common, making their friendship if not intimate, genuine, and mutually stimulating. In their distinct ways both men were social Darwinists who accepted the idea of struggle as necessary and proper to progress, optimistic that man would treat evils which were considered inevitable yesterday to be altogether

---

[43] Ibid.

[44] Ibid.

[45] Roosevelt to Lee, Oct. 16, 1906, Lee Papers.

[46] Roosevelt to Lee, Nov. 5, 1906, ibid. Lee previously had written to Roosevelt of Durand. "I hope you will like Sir Mortimer Durand and that he will prove a success. Personally, I know nothing of him at all and my only fear is that he may have made diplomacy too much of a profession." Lee to Roosevelt, Nov. 22, 1903, Roosevelt Papers.

[47] Roosevelt to Bryce, Nov. 27, 1908, Bryce Papers.

[48] Roosevelt to Bryce, late, 1908, ibid.

intolerable today. In addition Bryce and Roosevelt were supremely conscious of the similarities of Anglo-American institutions, the American republic issuing from English antecedents. As men of action, however, they were eager to translate their ideas into political realities, to promote the common good of the two peoples by a friendly but patriotic quest of their own country's best interest.

Roosevelt first met Bryce while the English savant was touring the United States gathering materials for a commentary on American politics which he planned to write. He immediately recognized in young Roosevelt a source of observation and information on the American scene, the kind of first-hand, informed yet candid opinion, that would explain the operation as well as the structure of the American system of governments. Roosevelt supplied Bryce with a great deal of comment on women suffrage, ethnic assimilation, religious affiliation, and civil service reform.[49] He sent him schedules of congressional bills, hoping they "meet your requirements. If not, or if you want additional information of any kind or sort, pray, write me at once."[50] Besides official reports, and in response to Bryce's requests, he passed along anecdotes and offhand observations. "For instance," he told Bryce,

I happen to know that the Ohio Republican Campaign Committee in its attempts to collect money for the prosecution of the campaign in Ohio this year from Government clerks in Washington received but a couple of thousand dollars. Under the old system they would probably have gotten ten thousand dollars by sheer blackmail.

And, he added, "you can use this information just as you wish."[51] TR read some of the galley proofs of the first edition of *The American Commonwealth*, complete with his own marginal critique. And he made a prediction.

I think your book will mark an epoch as distinctly as that of De Tocqueville. . . . I think everyone must be struck by the singular success with which you have combined a perfectly friendly spirit to America with an exact truthfulness both of statement and comment.[52]

The reception of *The American Commonwealth* and the reputation it won marked a fulfillment of Roosevelt's estimate.

In the 1890's the Bryce-Roosevelt friendship ripened. TR continued to advise Bryce about revisions in his book, but their exchange of ideas now included discussion of the westward movement of the Anglo-

American peoples across the world, a major phase of which Roosevelt had described in his own *The Winning of the West*. When the first volume appeared he promptly dispatched a copy to Bryce.[53] The Venezuelan boundary dispute of 1895–1896, straining Anglo-American diplomatic relations, also provided a topic pressing for discussion between the two friends. Bryce preferred to becalm the troubled atmosphere. Writing to Roosevelt early in 1896 about the "war scare" he expressed astonishment at the "apparent existence of ill-will towards Britain in a large part of your population. What in the world is the reason? There is nothing but friendliness on this side." Whereupon he proceeded to explain the position of his country in the controversy, taking direct issue with the American stand. Yet the total effect of Bryce's letter was friendly disagreement, which ended slyly: "But you really must not go to war with us—for then how should we be able to come and go and have our talks?"[54] The storm clouds of 1896 passed and under favorable skies the friendly talks were soon renewed.

Bryce made his fifth trip to the United States in 1897; he planned to visit Theodore Roosevelt who had been named assistant navy secretary in the spring of that year. Bryce had in mind one of those talks that would encompass the full catalog "of your political phenomena" "furnishing some opportunities for a persistent optimist like myself to show that he is not lightly discouraged."[55] Whatever the source of Bryce's misgivings in 1897 his appreciation of the world situation and the state of Anglo-American affairs in the wake of the Spanish-American War seemed brighter by 1898, though he was concerned about the possible internal effects of the American experiment in colonialism. "Our hearty congratulations on your safe return and on the laurels you have won." "How stupendous a change in the world these six months have brought." "It is a happy result . . . that your people and ours seem nearer together in sympathy than ever before."[56] These were all sentiments agreeable to Roosevelt. By the time Bryce assumed his ambassadorial post in 1907 events had provided London and Washington with numerous occasions for friendly understanding and cooperation, though there had been uneasy moments as well. As between Roosevelt and his other correspondents, trust and confidence became the established order in dealings between Bryce and TR. Bryce's biographer, H.A.L. Fisher, related how in 1901 the two men spent an evening together in the White House during which the president "opened his mind upon the subject of the Trusts." Bryce argued that trusts were but an offspring of the tariff and suggested that the evil be attacked at its root. The new president accepted the diagnosis but not the prescription, for as he pointed out to his guest

[49] Roosevelt to Bryce, Nov. 20, 1887, *ibid*. See also, Roosevelt, 1913: p. 89.
[50] Roosevelt to Bryce, Dec. 26, 1891, Bryce Papers.
[51] Roosevelt to Bryce, Dec. 26, 1891, Roosevelt Papers.
[52] Roosevelt to Bryce, Oct. 5, 1887, *Roosevelt Letters* 1: p. 134. For examples of the considerable exchange of information related to Bryce's book see: Roosevelt to Bryce, Nov., 1896, to Bryce, Nov. 12, 1897, Bryce Papers; Bryce to Roosevelt, Feb. 28, 1891, to Roosevelt, Dec. 12, 1891, to Roosevelt, Feb. 25, 1895, Roosevelt Papers.

[53] Roosevelt to Bryce, Nov. 13, 1891, Bryce Papers.
[54] Bryce to Roosevelt, Jan. 1, 1896, *ibid*.
[55] Bryce to Roosevelt, July 7, 1897, Roosevelt Papers.
[56] Bryce to Roosevelt, Sept. 12, 1898, *ibid*.

he did not possess the political power to wage war on the trusts and the tariff simultaneously. This kind of frank and confidential discussion later typified their dealings when Bryce was ambassador.[57]

James Bryce served in Washington from February, 1907, to April, 1913. His aim as ambassador was threefold: to cultivate the good will of the American people at large; to settle whatever outstanding differences there were between Britain and the United States; and to leave behind a structural framework which would facilitate harmonious relations between the two countries in the future.[58] In all these objectives he received the official cooperation of Theodore Roosevelt as president and his moral support after he left office. Even before TR departed the White House, Bryce managed to resolve several lesser but troublesome issues: a final boundary line between Canada and the United States and the regulation of fisheries on their inland contiguous waters among them. More significant, the president and the ambassador saw eye to eye on the role of the Anglo-American nations relative to the world situation. "I am delighted to see what a splendid reception your navy has had in Australia," Bryce informed the president as "the great white fleet" plowed the Pacific. "It seems to me that one of the best results of this wonderful voyage has been the heartiness of the greetings exchanged between your sailors and our own people."[59] Via Bryce Roosevelt undertook to communicate certain private American reports on conditions in India and China to the London government, indicative of his interest in maintaining British power in those areas. Similarily the ambassador had nothing but praise for the president's speech, "The Expansion of the White Race," which paraded the good effects for civilization of British conquests in the East and voiced the hope that Britain would preserve a tradition of imperialism.[60] "Let me thank you again," Bryce wrote, "for that admirable speech you made last night to the Methodists. I have never seen the case for missionary effort as it stands today put either with more force or with more perfect truth and insight. What you said about Africa as well as about India is most sound and most helpful."[61] Bryce also conveyed the warm endorsement of Sir Edward Grey, adding that what had been said would be "most highly appreciated both in England and in India."[62] Replying to

these compliments, the president wrote pointedly: "If I have been of the least use in the matter, I am more than pleased."[63]

During his Afro-European trip, 1909–1910, Roosevelt kept in touch with Bryce. From Naples he reported: "I have been in rather stormy petrel condition ever since I left Khartoum. I hardly need say how deeply appreciative I am of all the courtesy shown me by your officials. It was rather difficult to remember I was not at home."[64] At journey's end the ambassador sent a "welcome home" note, telling of his pleasure that TR's bird walk with Earl Grey in the New Forest "came off" and congratulating him on the Romanes Lecture which, he remarked, "seems to have been as warmly appreciated as I felt it would be."[65] In the same year, 1910, another edition of *The American Commonwealth* appeared, a copy of which Bryce sent along to Roosevelt. Much of the intellectual brotherhood and common purpose these men shared was present in TR's letter of thanks.

The two volumes of your work—your great classic work —have come. How well I remember nearly thirty years ago, when as a very young man in the New York Legislature, I, at your request, went over some of the proof of the first edition. Well, I am glad you feel as you say in your preface that things have grown a little better, rather than a little worse, during these thirty years. There is much that is evil, much that is menacing for the future. That is the way I feel about it myself. And there are points in which we are worse off than we were thirty years ago; but, on the whole, I think we stand ahead and not behind where we then stood.[66]

The 1914 war soon cast serious doubts over the future, just as it placed no little burden on the relations of Bryce and the former president.

Once Theodore Roosevelt became convinced of the immorality of German policies in bringing on the war and in executing a military campaign to implement those policies, he was loudly insistent that the United States join forces with England and France against a common foe. From the Bryce Report detailing German excesses Roosevelt obtained ample ammunition to keep up his attacks on the Germans as agents of destruction and doom. The British government, and Bryce himself to some extent, were much more concerned with cultivating the Wilson administration, whose posture toward the war TR dismissed as craven and hypocritical, than the support, moral or vocal, of an ex-president.[67] Once the United States came into the

[57] Fischer, 1920: 1: pp. 6–7.

[58] For a discerning account of James Bryce as British ambassador to the United States see, Peter Neary, 1965.

[59] Bryce to Roosevelt, Aug. 27, 1908, Bryce Papers. Roosevelt wrote to George O. Trevelyan that he was "extremely pleased" by the voyage and by the reception accorded the American navy in Australia. Roosevelt to Trevelyan, Nov. 6, 1908, *Roosevelt Letters* 6: p. 1330.

[60] Roosevelt, "The Expansion of the White Race," *Works* 18: pp. 341–354.

[61] Bryce to Roosevelt, Jan. 20, 1909, Bryce Papers.

[62] Bryce to Roosevelt, Jan. 20, 1909, *ibid.* (This was a second letter written the same day about the same speech.)

[63] Roosevelt to Bryce, Jan. 21, 1909, *Roosevelt Letters* 6: p. 1478. Lee wrote of the speech. "I can't tell you what wholehearted pleasure your tribute to our work in India has given to everyone with whom I have come in contact since, and moreover you chose a moment to say what you did which made your testimony of quite peculiar value to us." Lee to Roosevelt, Jan. 29, 1909, Roosevelt Papers.

[64] Roosevelt to Bryce, April 2, 1910, Bryce Papers.

[65] Bryce to Roosevelt, June 19, 1910, *ibid.*

[66] Roosevelt to Bryce, June 10 ,1911, *ibid.*

[67] Roosevelt to Bryce, May 29, 1915, *ibid.*

war the Roosevelt-Bryce friendship began to run a smooth course once more, on personal as well as policy levels. In March, 1917, Bryce commented on the pending state of war between the United States and Germany: "Needless to tell you this has long seemed to be practically unavoidable and desirable in the interests of mankind."[68] In October of that year he wrote to TR:

We hear that your sons are going to the Front in France. If they pass through England, or come across on leave to England, I trust you will let us know, that we may come and see them again and put them in touch with some people in England they would like to know and who would like to know them.[69]

Both old friends looked forward to peace, anxious that it should be achieved with victory, but somewhat apprehensive about the portending postwar radicalism.[70]

St. Loe Strachey, editor of the *Spectator,* was another prominent Englishman, vigorous in his espousal of Anglo-Americanism, with whom Theodore Roosevelt developed a deep feeling of kinship and understanding. He and TR began corresponding in the later 1890's, and as Strachey and his wife planned to visit America in 1899 Roosevelt invited them to see him in Albany. The visit did not take place until 1902, but in the intervening years through their letters they got to know and like each other. Strachey himself was rampantly pro-American, a voice calling for cooperation between the two leading English-speaking peoples on all fronts, from the day he assumed editorship of the *Spectator* in 1898.

Any number of Strachey's ideas and proposals made him attractive to TR. By background he was in the imperialist tradition, his great grandfather having served as secretary to Clive in India, and through the pages of the *Spectator* he sought always to strengthen imperialist ties. He was also an energetic proponent of military preparedness on a voluntary basis with individual citizens willing to train in military fashion out of a sense of loyalty and duty to country. Strachey set up his own Volunteer Company in Surrey as early as 1906, a practice that was so widely imitated in the years down to the First World War that in 1914 the War Office had a list of 250,000 trained men, thanks largely to the idea original with Strachey. As he once wrote to the president: "the purpose of four months or so of training would be to make a 'full man.' No man is a 'full man' unless he knows how to defend his home and country."[71] Finally Strachey was strongly anti-socialist, thoughts on which he exchanged on numerous occasions with Roosevelt. The sympathies of the two men were really quite extensive. The individualistic strain in their thinking doubtlessly drew them together which, when combined with a genuine admiration each

held for the other's homeland, brought along their friendship.

Strachey's editorship of the *Spectator* imparted curious aspects to his relationship with Roosevelt, especially while the latter was in high public office. Critics of Anglo-American accord, especially in the early years of the twentieth century, were vocal and powerful on both sides of the Atlantic. Strachey realized that he had carefully to weigh his words in print, lest sensibility and prejudice be offended. In September, 1901, for example, he wrote TR saying that he hoped what he had written in the *Spectator* on the death of McKinley would not be judged too cold and unsympathetic. "I felt more warmly than I wrote, but I was anxious not to slop over and so be misunderstood on your side. . . . Knowing what harm is done in your country by anything which seems to ticket a man as a friend of England, I was careful to give no occasion for such misunderstanding." In the same letter he adds he was "only speaking the honest truth" in agreement with most Englishmen, that the one real consolation was the belief that "the executive office would fall into worthy hands."[72] The new president's reply gave indication of the future direction of his dealings with Strachey. "Now, if I had time I would write you with entire freedom and at great length on many subjects, for, my dear sir, though I have never met you, you are one of the men to whom I am willing to write with the most absolute confidence. . . ."[73] The effusiveness of Roosevelt's words do not destroy their sincerity as his subsequent letters to Strachey attest.

The president invited the Stracheys to stay with him at the White House for part of their American tour which took place in the autumn of 1902. Their two-day stay with Roosevelt, occupying a room that had been used by John Hay during Lincoln's time—a fact that deeply stirred Strachey—was the high point of their American visit. Upon being introduced to them, President Roosevelt said: "I am very, very glad to see you," and a kinship that had its source in letters took on a more affecting quality. During the reception that followed this introduction Roosevelt and his guests were soon completely at ease and before long were discussing with force and candor the pros and cons of the Alaska boundary controversy. The next morning the president took Strachey with him into the executive office and once more they fell into earnest conversation. Before Strachey realized it the room had filled with cabinet officers and a cabinet session had spontaneously commenced. With some embarrassment Strachey turned to John Hay and excused himself. That afternoon, as Strachey was an expert and indefatigible horseman, he and the president made a hard ride to the

[68] Bryce to Roosevelt, March 21, 1917, *ibid.*

[69] Bryce to Roosevelt, Oct. 25, 1917, *ibid.*

[70] For example, Roosevelt to Bryce, Nov. 26, 1917, to Bryce, Aug. 7, 1918; Bryce to Roosevelt, Oct. 30, 1918, *ibid.*

[71] Strachey to Roosevelt, March 10, 1906, Strachey Papers.

[72] Strachey to Roosevelt, Sept. 23, 1901, *ibid.* Strachey had confided to Roosevelt that "the truth is I like to keep the American articles in the *Spectator* whenever possible in my own hands." Strachey to Roosevelt, Dec. 29, 1904, Roosevelt Papers.

[73] Roosevelt to Strachey, Oct. 15, 1901, Strachey Papers.

suburbs and their saddle talk did not end until dusk. Writing to thank his host a few days later St. Loe Strachey called the White House sojourn "the greatest of honours," and unable to resist a political jibe, added, "an infinitely greater honour than to stop at the Winter Palace or the Hofburg. *There is no comparison.*" [74] Years later he was to call this meeting with Roosevelt "one of the most delightful memories" of his life. [75] In 1910 the Stracheys were able to repay the presidential hospitality while Roosevelt was in London. They arranged an intimate dinner for him that included only Lord and Lady Cromer, and Sir Cecil Spring Rice and his wife. The talk that night moved from current politics to the principles of self-government within the British empire. So much of what Strachey and Roosevelt had discussed over the years in their letters came into focus; so much of what they would write each other in the days ahead was better understood and appreciated because of this brief, personal encounter. [76]

Before 1910 the Roosevelt-Strachey correspondence displayed several recurring themes. Socialism was among the most prominent. Both men agreed that one of the forces making for socialist appeal to the masses was the irresponsibility of the capitalist class which for its own aggrandizement fostered trusts and tariffs. Roosevelt's opposition to the trusts, carefully orchestrated as it was to the beat of politics, was nonetheless authentic. In Strachey's judgment TR gave the "lead to all those here as well as in America who are determined on the one hand to fight socialism, and on the other to hold the trusts and the combines in check. That the victory in the end will be yours and ours," he insisted to Roosevelt, "I do not doubt because right, common sense, and the conscience of mankind are with us." [77] He wrote at length to the president about a lecture he had given on "Society and the Family" to a University Extension gathering at Oxford. A good many of the audience, he related, were "genuine working men and others were school masters and school mistresses in elementary schools."

I am sorry to say I found a great majority of my audience strong Socialists. They were however a very straight forward, good sort of people, and in the hours discussion which followed the lecture, I think I was able to make some impression upon them and to make them face the destruction of the family which must follow the adoption of such measures as (1) universal, unearned old age pensions; (2) the endowment of motherhood; (3) feeding of all school children by the State; (4) the endowment of unemployment. Only one or two wild socialists were willing to say that if the family and socialism were in conflict, so much the worse for the family. [78]

In reply Roosevelt agreed. "I was greatly interested in your article on socialism and I was even more pleased with your letter. It is curious how exactly you and I agree on most of the great questions which are fundamentally the same in both countries." [79] In 1907–1908 Strachey published in the *Spectator* a series of "Letters to a working Man," setting forth his views of "the perils and problems" of Socialism. He planned to bring the series together in booklet form and sought TR's permission to dedicate the collected essays to him, a request the president granted. [80] "I have a special reason for making the request," he wrote.

I have of course been accused, because I wrote against Socialism, of being a hard-hearted supporter of Capital and the rich. . . . If I dedicate this book to you I shall bring home to people in a striking way that the enemies of Socialism are also the enemies of unrestrained Capitalism. I regard you, the opponent of Trusts and evil finances and selfish exploitation of the masses, as the greatest supporter tions to their common problems. [82]

The common destiny of the Anglo-American peoples was bound up in Strachey's mind with common solution to their common problems. [82]

During these same years, 1902–1910, the Roosevelt-Strachey friendship also became more personal. A second American voyage set for the fall of 1907 during which the two men planned to visit was forestalled by the death of Strachey's first son who succumbed to pneumonia while a student at Balliol. His letter of March 25, 1907, telling the president the sad news betrayed the deep kinship that had grown up between them. [83] In the same spirit Strachey both telegraphed and wrote his sympathy to TR and the American people upon learning of the San Francisco earthquake. [84] At another level, Roosevelt and Strachey exchanged private views of William Randolph Hearst and the English journalist, Edward Dicey, each willing to abide in the adverse judgment by the other. [85]

World War I had a solidifying effect on the Roosevelt-Strachey friendship. As with Arthur Lee, no recriminations came about between TR and the editor of the *Spectator* over what America ought to do about the war. By March, 1915, Roosevelt was writing Strachey that it was "utterly futile to be favorable to the Allies and yet uphold the [Wilson] administration," an attitude his English friend was in the fullest agree-

[74] Strachey to Roosevelt, Oct. 29, 1902, Roosevelt Papers. (Italics in original.)

[75] Strachey to Roosevelt, Nov. 24, 1904, *ibid.*

[76] For an interesting description of the Stracheys at the White House see Amy Strachey, 1930: pp. 135–137.

[77] Strachey to Roosevelt, Aug. 26, 1906, Roosevelt Papers.

[78] *Ibid.*

[79] Roosevelt to Strachey, Sept. 8, 1907, *Roosevelt Letters* 5: p. 768.

[80] Roosevelt to Strachey, March 14, 1908, *ibid.* 6: p. 971.

[81] Strachey to Roosevelt, March 4, 1908, Roosevelt Papers.

[82] See also, Roosevelt to Strachey, Feb. 22, 1907, *Roosevelt Letters,* 5: p. 596, to Strachey, Sept. 16, 1904, Strachey Papers; to Strachey, Dec. 4, 1904, *ibid;* to Strachey, Sept. 11, 1905, *ibid;* also Strachey to Roosevelt, April 3, 1906, *ibid;* to Roosevelt, Jan. 3, 1908, Roosevelt Papers.

[83] Strachey to Roosevelt, March 25, 1907, Roosevelt Papers.

[84] Strachey to Roosevelt, April 23, 1906, Roosevelt Papers.

[85] Roosevelt to Strachey, Oct. 25, 1906, *Roosevelt Letters 5*: p. 468; Strachey to Roosevelt, June 22, 1908, Roosevelt Papers.

ment with.[86] Both men saw German victory as a threat to their common culture and their common advantage.[87]

George Otto Trevelyan and Theodore Roosevelt were attracted to each other by reason of temperament and taste. Their fondness for history alone might have accomplished the friendship. Each man made history, Roosevelt in a remarkable way; each wrote history, Trevelyan with distinction. Through history they became imbued with the meaning of Anglo-American unity. Trevelyan's *The American Revolution* was a fairer presentation of the war for independence than had been offered theretofore by an English scholar; TR's *The Winning of the West* glorified conquest by the Anglo-Americans and placed that movement within the larger parameters of "the world movement" by men speaking English in the eighteenth and nineteenth centuries.

Like Bryce, Trevelyan was twenty years Theodore Roosevelt's senior and by the time they had commenced their correspondence he had already retired from public life in order to pursue his literary and historical vocation. He served in Parliament for many years and was a member of Gladstone's first ministry as civil lord of the Admiralty. While in the Commons in the 1870's he was known as a strenuous advocate of the working class franchise and held various cabinet posts as well. In all of this he had come to know many of the leading figures in English politics and to be in close touch with men like Lord Roseberry, John Morley, James Bryce, and Edward Grey. His friendship with Roosevelt was built upon history in the making as well as the written record. In his writings to TR, Trevelyan relied upon experience as much as anything to promote a growing understanding with Roosevelt and the American people. In these letters he alluded to Gladstone or Morley just as though his friend in America knew and viewed these persons as he did, drawing out the subtleties of Anglo-American unity.

Whatever direction their correspondence took, by whatever thoughts their friendship was cemented, this unity was discernible. Their liking for John Morley depicted this. Of Morley, Trevelyan had spoken to Roosevelt:

For ten years I sat next to Morley in the House of Commons and it was a great anti-dote to the dreariness and bad rhetoric which was the prevailing atmosphere of that, as I suppose of all national assemblies. I have never heard from him a sentence, or read from him a letter that was dull or common.[88]

And Roosevelt responded with much the same estimate.

. . . Morley spent three or four days with us and I found him as delightful a companion as one could wish to have, and I quite understand the comfort he must have been to

you when you sat beside him in the House of Commons. Incidentally it is rather a relief to have you speak as you do about the tedious and trivial quality of most of the eloquence in the House. I am glad to find that it is characteristic of all parliamentary bodies and not merely that of my own country.[89]

The effect of such a good humored exchange is to recognize that Trevelyan and Roosevelt really did see themselves as kinsmen, a condition re-enforced by mutual friends and common institutional experiences.

In their correspondence Roosevelt and Trevelyan spoke of Thackeray or Dickens, of Hawthorne or Poe, feeling they shared a common past; of James II, of Philip of Spain or Jefferson Davis, confident they enjoyed a common prejudice.[90] They mourned together the death of John Hay, refought the battles of the American Revolution and the Spanish-American War. And they compared political systems.[91] Roosevelt wrote to Trevelyan, by way of commenting on the cabinet form of government: "it is not possible for the politicians to throw over the real party leader and put up as a dummy some grey tinted person . . . or at least though perhaps it is possible, the opportunity and the temptation are much less than in the American system.[92] Trevelyan made a useful distinction in reply. "With regard to what you say of the differences between us and you in the selection of the man who is to govern, I should express it by saying that in America, the country elects the *ruler,* and in England, the country elects the *party.*"[93] These two friends were supremely aware of the importance of the character of the men who operated through party or ruled in the nation. Their moral camaraderie was again evident. "It does not seem to me that it is fair to say that passionate earnestness and self-devotion, delicateness of conscience and lofty aim are likely to prove a hindrance instead of a help to a statesman or a politician. Of course," as Roosevelt continued to explain himself to his confidant, "if he has no balance of common sense, then the man will go to pieces; but it will be because he is a fool, not because he has some qualities of a moral hero."[94] Trevelyan's agreement utilized germane examples.

---

[86] Roosevelt to Strachey, March 23, 1915, Strachey Papers.
[87] Their views are fully developed in chapter 4.
[88] Trevelyan to Roosevelt, Nov. 10, 1904, Roosevelt Papers.

[89] Roosevelt to Trevelyan, Nov. 24, 1904, Bishop, 1920: 2: p. 144.
[90] Roosevelt to Tervelyan, Nov. 24, 1904, *ibid*, p. 144; Trevelyan to Roosevelt, Dec. 8, 1904, Roosevelt Papers; Roosevelt to Trevelyan, Jan. 22, 1906, *ibid;* Trevelyan to Roosevelt, Jan. 8, 1906, *ibid.*
[91] Trevelyan to Roosevelt, July 15, 1905, Bishop, 1920: 2: pp. 150–152; Roosevelt to Trevelyan, Sept 12, 1905, *Roosevelt Letters* 5: pp. 22–25; Trevelyan to Roosevelt, Nov. 27, 1907, Bishop, 1920: 2: pp. 165–166; Roosevelt to Trevelyan, Jan. 1, 1908, *Rooseevlt Letters* 6: pp. 880–883; Trevelyan to Roosevelt, Jan. 18, 1908, Bishop, 1920; 2: pp. 171–172.
[92] Roosevelt to Trevelyan, May 28, 1904, *Roosevelt Letters* 5: p. 806.
[93] Trevelyan to Roosevelt, Nov. 10, 1904, Bishop, 1920: 2: p. 143. (Italics in original.)
[94] Roosevelt to Trevelyan, Sept. 12, 1905, *Roosevelt Letters* 5: p. 24.

Washington ... prevented a terrible war with England in 1795 at the cost of a great part of his popularity and at a time in life when his enormous personal position and moral dignity by which he was so universally and for so long surrounded wherever his name was known, rendered the brutalities and vulgarities of political detraction as directed against him, humiliating and almost grotesque. Lincoln, again under immense temptation and difficulties, prevented another desolating war with us at the time of the *Trent*.[95]

To prevent wars between America and England was to balance morality with common sense in a way that Anglo-Americans of the twentieth century especially could appreciate.

The Roosevelt-Trevelyan friendship had a more personal side as well. When Trevelyan's eldest son, Charles, was in the United States in 1897, TR befriended him and through him sent an invitation for Sir George to visit the United States. "I am glad to thank you for your great kindness to my son," came the answer. "Your extraordinary attention to a young stranger when you were Secretary to the Admiralty greatly struck one who had been a Secretary to the Admiralty himself." But he declined Roosevelt's invitation, saying: "I am getting too old for going to America ... but I am not too old to enjoy the feeling of sympathy with such a career as yours. I expect a great deal more of that pleasure before our common sojourn on this planet is over."[96] To speak his gratitude Trevelyan sent Roosevelt a copy of the first volume of *The American Revolution*. Their personal values, their taste for literature and history, and their passion for politics had combined from the start to launch a friendship.[97]

In December, 1907, the president along with Henry Cabot Lodge and Elihu Root sent a silver loving cup to Trevelyan with the inscription: "To the Historian of the American Revolution from his friends—Theodore Roosevelt, Henry Cabot Lodge, and Elihu Root." In this way they sought to acknowledge in a personal way the volumes describing the war for American independence which had appeared down to 1907. Trevelyan's answer told of his "pleasure and pride" at receiving the gift. "The cup is a noble piece," he wrote, "and the simplicity and singular beauty of proportion struck us much and impressed us with the notion that there must be much artistic feeling among the silver workers in America."[98] During TR's 1910 visit to England he and Sir George spent a quiet afternoon together at "Welcombe," Stratford on Avon, where the Trevelyans regularly summered. Looking back to that afternoon from the vantage point of somber days in World War I, Trevelyan recalled that Roosevelt's visit to "Wel-

combe" "always will be to me the greatest memory connected with it."[99] After returning to the United States, Roosevelt in 1911 gave a full account of his Afro-European tour in a famous letter to Sir George.[100] In the next year, when news reached England of the attempt on the ex-president's life in the 1912 Bull Moose campaign, Trevelyan wrote at once: "I have been unable to forebear sending you a few lines; although perhaps I should have waited. This matter has given me the full measure of the personal affection which I bear towards you."[101] The 1914 war drew Roosevelt and Trevelyan even closer together They agreed completely on the moral issue of the conflict, and were committed to the battle in the persons of their sons.[102] When two of TR's boys were wounded Trevelyan wrote in concern and sympathy. Roosevelt acknowledged his appreciation in what was the most suitable way for him by praising the "high and gallant valor" of George Trevelyan *fils* who was himself on active service.[103] By then Roosevelt had become to the older Trevelyan "the best and closest friend I have made in the evening of my life, when a man is very seldom fortunate enough to make such a friend."[104] On such a note the friendship closed in 1919 with the death of Theodore Roosevelt. Of the five major English correspondents, only Cecil Spring Rice predeceased TR, but not before he and the others, Lee and Bryce, Strachey and Trevelyan, had lived to witness America committed to England and the Allies in a test and a proof of an alliance, to the building of which they, by their friendships, had contributed.

II. COMMITMENTS

Theodore Roosevelt felt a personal attraction to his English friends and they to him, an undeniably important aspect of their relations with each other. Yet individually he was as fond of the German ambassador, Speck von Sternburg or Jules Jusserand, the French diplomat, as certain of his English friends, so that attraction to the latter group either anticipated deeper intellectual commitments or else grew from a mutual recognition of the common heritage of the Anglo-American peoples. The rapprochement did not derive from personalities who happened to be agreeable one to another and thus likely to conform their views of priorities or policies. As influential as men may be on events, as much direction as Roosevelt and his friends conceivably exerted on the affairs of their nations—and admittedly the extent of influence exercised by the

---

[95] Trevelyan to Roosevelt, Sept. 25, 1905, Roosevelt Papers.
[96] Trevelyan to Roosevelt, Jan. 27, 1899, *ibid*.
[97] Upon receipt of TR's thank-you note, Trevelyan wrote at the bottom: "This is the hero! I suppose he will some day be President. I sent the book to him as he was so kind to Charles." See Bishop, 1920, **2**: p. 139.
[98] Trevelyan to Roosevelt, Jan. 8, 1908, Roosevelt Papers.

[99] Trevelyan to Roosevelt, Jan. 8, 1915, *ibid*.
[100] Roosevelt to Trevelyan, Oct. 1, 1911, *Roosevelt Letters* **5**: pp. 348–415.
[101] Trevelyan to Roosevelt, Oct. 18, 1912, Roosevelt Papers.
[102] Trevelyan to Roosevelt, May 13, 1915, *ibid;* Roosevelt to Trevelyan, May 29, 1915, *ibid*.
[103] Trevelyan to Roosevelt, March 31, 1918, *ibid;* Roosevelt to Trevelyan, April 9, 1918, Bishop, 1920: **2**: p. 181.
[104] Trevelyan to Roosevelt, May 14, 1912, Roosevelt Papers; see also Roosevelt to Trevelyan, Jan. 8, 1915, *ibid*.

several Englishmen TR knew best was limited—hardly warrants such an assertion. These friendships had their complement in common but distinct national purposes, whereas Roosevelt's liking for Baron von Sternburg did not, because the origin of America had been basically British, because American institutions consciously traced their beginnings back to England, because a majority of the American population and an overwhelming percentage of the ruling class was of British stock. Great Britain and the United States by 1900 had become increasingly aware of their likenesses and equally prone to overlook past animosities. Events may have forced them to make this adjustment, England's dangerous isolation, America's search for a *weltpolitik*. The rush of events was channeled by a sense of identity between the English and American peoples, portrayed in the correspondence of Roosevelt and his friends as commitments which as individuals they keenly felt.

Their correspondence disclosed an ethnic awareness and a general cultural sympathy, emphasizing the organic kinship of American and English political institutions and the values informing those institutions. It also revealed a consciousness of a great historical past shared by both nations and a studied deliberation of what the future held for the Anglo-American race. These letters spoke a justification of the use of force to maintain the leadership the two nations enjoyed, a belief that force had been a critical element in achieving their world position. Force was not often avowed for its own sake but rather to promote some noble purpose like "the spread of civilization," or "the planting of institutions of self-government" across the wastelands of the world. This kind of reasoning must always seem like the smuggest of rationalizations, for it presumed the superiority, whether innate or acquired, of the Anglo-American way of life. It had its source in that set of principles that included the tenets that God was an English gentleman, the Anglo-Americans his chosen race, the English law his dispensation. While neither Roosevelt nor his friends subscribed to the testament fully or succumbed to its grosser temptations they did believe in themselves as world leaders and proposed to concert together in an effort to maintain their hegemony. Spring Rice spoke this view perfectly in writing to Edith Carow Roosevelt in 1905 from Berlin. In describing the Kaiser to her, he commented:

He is a man of great ideas . . . but I believe wrong ideas, because they are based on pure selfishness. You know I don't think *your* patriotism enlarged selfishness because the base of it is—to make one's own nation play that part in the world's work which it was made for, and to do it well—and to help other nations to do theirs—and to promote good feeling and the happiness of nations.[1]

In so saying, Spring Rice demonstrated that the Anglo-Americans possessed what they conceived to be a perfectly logical, perfectly coherent rationale. Grounded on a certain racial uniqueness, it had been shown by history to be a reality and no mere abstraction, it functioned effectively in the world of 1900, and it provided the populace with a purpose transcending the individual in the name of the nation and of humanity. It was nineteenth-century nationalism at its most explicit, and Theodore Roosevelt as well as his English friends were all committed to it as a formidable dynamic.

In their exchange of thoughts the correspondents did not address themselves with equal attention to all the elements of the rationale of commitment, though TR himself offered his views on virtually every aspect of the common inheritance. Bryce and Roosevelt, for example, tended to discuss political forms or the function of law, Strachey, the values which men ought to live by, Spring Rice, the meaning of "Anglo-America" and the destiny of the people who spoke English. Such distinctions are useful and appropriate to make, yet in the overview an intellectual cross-fertilization of such complexity occurred as to disclose the range and capacity not only of Theodore Roosevelt but of his correspondents also.

Englishmen and Americans alike pride themselves on their forms of government, a logical starting place in the circle of common ideas which helped to join together what Roosevelt called "our two great peoples . . . the only two really free great peoples."[2] It was TR's friend, James Bryce, who wrote the most celebrated treatise on American political ways since de Tocqueville. America was worthy of Bryce's adventurous spirit just as its republican form of government was worthy of his intellectual curiosity. He wrote *The American Commonwealth* as an Anglo-American. The political phenomenon of America fascinated him because it had grown from English precedents and pursuantly established English political ways over this vital area of the world. Bryce's accomplishment was not the result of mere pride in America but of hard work in gathering data and impressions from every part of the nation he had brought under his scrutiny. His inquiry depended on the minds of many others for assistance. A long and distinguished list of collaborators included not only Theodore Roosevelt but Oliver Wendell Holmes, Jr., Albert Shaw, John Hay, Seth Low, Henry Charles Lea, to choose at random from Bryce's acknowledgments in the Preface to the first edition of his book. In particular, Roosevelt was an enthusiastic and valuable source of information because his own feel for history and mastery of facts opened up to Bryce precisely the kind of mind that supplied the statistics of the moment along

---

[1] Spring Rice to Edith Carew Roosevelt, Mar. 29, 1905, Gwynn, 1929: 1: p. 467. For an evaluation of TR's attitude toward various diplomats see Nelson Blake, "Ambassadors at

the Court of Theodore Roosevelt," *Miss. Valley Hist. Rev.* 42 (1955–1956): pp. 179–206.

[2] Roosevelt to Lee, Aug. 4, 1900, Roosevelt Papers.

with an awareness of how the American present had developed. In giving Bryce information on nineteenth-century immigration, for example, Roosevelt made use of the history of the eighteenth century as a source of insight for understanding the later situation. Writing of conditions that existed a hundred years earlier he observed:

As regards the German (rather the German and Dutch) element in the colonies it is curious how little is known of the matter generally. Remember that nowadays New England and the South are still free from immigrants, or non-English speaking people (passing by the Irish in the former) as I said this ethnic element *is* a new one. The older foreign element existed only in the middle and western states.

But this is precisely as it was a century ago. We of course have no accurate race statistics of that time. But at least one third of Pennsylvania was German; there were many Swedes, Dutch and Germans in Delaware; also in New Jersey and New York in 1776 there were 11 regular churches—2 Church of England, 3 Presbyterian, 2 German, 3 Dutch and 1 French Huguenot. There were large German settlements in the valley of the Mohawk, except Long Island, but a few of our farmers were then of English blood. The great German societies in New York used German until about the beginning of the present century in their reports, etc., they then took up English; but about 1840 again went back to German. . . . The older Germans assimilated slower than do the Germans of today.[3]

Such discussion tended to appeal to Bryce's historical sensitivity which in turn was evident in his treatment of the assimilation of various groups in contemporary America and the prospects of future immigration.[4]

As Bryce made revisions of his book he and Roosevelt remained in touch. From TR he received official reports of the Civil Service Commission at a time when Roosevelt was a member of that body as the "best answer [to] most of your questions as to the progress of civil service reform in the past five or six years." Bryce profited from his offhand comments as well.

You ask me if the regular spoilsmen are less audacious than the federal supervisors themselves in insisting on party and personal patronage. I don't think they are. I think in the country there is more bitter feeling among the regular spoilsmen of the Gorman and Ingalls type against the Civil Service Commission than ever before.[5]

Bryce, engaged in assessing the life of American politics along with its structure and history, got much appropriate commentary from TR. Alluding to the work of the 52nd Congress, for example, he observed that "the President and the Senate will prevent any revolutionary legislation." In commenting on the 1896 presidential election, one in which for TR, Bryan was a dangerous demogogue, he wrote Bryce: "the foreigners in the big cities went wrong more often than the native

Americans, but in the country at large this was not so. As a whole the Germans did markedly better than the native Americans; the Scandinavians quite as well; the Irish nearly as well."[6] Seeking to give his English friend still another perspective on the 1896 election he later wrote that the native American vote did not go for Bryan. "East of the Alleghenies and north of the Potomac, for example, the native American vote was cast for the Republican party."[7] All this Roosevelt saw as part of the larger process of Americanization, one of the many unique aspects of the American experience that exercised a fascination on observers like Bryce. Events confirmed the process in his judgment. With his former collaboration with Bryce obviously in mind he told his friend as the United States entered World War I: "You will be interested to know that I am perfectly certain that the great majority of Americans of German descent are exactly loyal as any other Americans."[8] Bryce's absorption in American political ways and the work of Roosevelt, along with many others, in supplying him with the requisite information, were natural, considering the kinship of the two nations. It was also typical of the knowledgeable political discussions found in Roosevelt's English correspondence.

No more arresting feature of the common political outlook shared by Roosevelt and his friends prevailed than their belief in the value of self-government. Successful self-government was the mark of the most advanced and gifted of peoples. How, in fact, was self-government achieved? Apart from similar political structures, yet essential to their development, was an underlying set of values, sometimes summed up as "the Whig temperament." Roosevelt often exchanged thoughts with Strachey regarding it. "A man who was moderate might nevertheless be as sternly resolute in his extreme conviction as any extreme fanatic," TR wrote Strachey as he reflected on the essence of Macaulay's *Essays*.[9] Strachey's view "exactly coincided" with his friend's. "After all why should not one hold the Whig spirit with enthusiasm as our forefathers did? Moderation and the happy mean have been justly applauded in all ages, and though they are far more difficult to attain than the extremes, they ought to call for the maximum devotion. After all," he continued, "liberty can and does only reside in moderation and the avoidance of violence and fanaticism."[10] At one point during his presidency Roosevelt was prompted to defend his record as a reformer in these terms in a letter to Trevelyan. ". . . As inevitably happens in any period of constructive legislation, we tend to alienate the extremes of both sides . . . radicals who think we have not gone far enough . . . reaction-

---

[3] Roosevelt to Bryce, Nov. 20, 1887, Bryce Papers.
[4] Bryce, 1897, 2: pp. 861 ff.
[5] Roosevelt to Bryce, Dec. 26, 1891, Bryce Papers.

[6] Roosevelt to Bryce, Nov. 18, 1896, *ibid.*
[7] Roosevelt to Bryce, March 12, 1897, *ibid.*
[8] Roosevelt to Bryce, April 19, 1917, *ibid.*
[9] Roosevelt to Strachey, Sept. 16, 1904, Strachey Papers.
[10] Strachey to Roosevelt, Oct. 1, 1904, Roosevelt Papers.

aries who think we have gone altogether too far." [11] Once referring to his involvement in the 1912 presidential race TR told St. Loe Strachey:

I am a man who believes with all fervor in moderate progress. Too often men who believe in moderation believe in it only moderately and tepidly, and leave fervor to the extremes of the two sides—the extremists of reaction and the extremists of progress. Washington, Lincoln, Chatham, the Whigs of the Reform Bill and Macaulay are men who, to my mind, stand as types of what wise, progressive leadership should be.[12]

In short, Roosevelt and his friends preferred the practical to the visionary, Lincoln to the Fifth Monarchy men.[13] Roosevelt insisted on the sanity of this principle and, in his own judgment at least, he adhered to it throughout his public career. Looking to the post-1918 era, which seemed pregnant with extremes and upheavals, he wrote to James Bryce:

I am a very radical democrat; and I grow more rather than less radical as I grow older; but I am equally radical in insisting on orderly liberty, and upon efficiency—*efficiency in the interests of the man who toils,* but not in the interests of the man who wishes reward of toil without toiling.[14]

Roosevelt's statement that he believed he had remained radically moderate stressed the importance he attached to this principle.

In matters of practical application the Whig temperament called for reliance on party, something critical to the Anglo-American political systems. Roosevelt's attitude toward party he stated well in a letter to the author of *The American Commonwealth.*

When I came back from Cuba in 1898, the Machine . . . took me up and nominated me. They would not have nominated me if I had not been a straight Republican, one who while always acting ultimately on his own best judgment and according to his own beliefs in right and wrong, was yet anxious always to consult with and if possible come to an agreement with party leaders. In other words I had what the Mugwump conspicuously lacks, and what the Frenchmen, and in fact all peoples who are unfitted for self-government lack, namely, the power of coming to a consensus with my fellows.[15]

Party was no less essential to his English friends than to Roosevelt. St. Loe Strachey, for example, referring to their common admiration for Macaulay, wrote:

Macaulay really loved liberty and hated cruelty and oppression, though he was always a good party man. As he chose the right party you and I will not think the worse of him for that. The more I live, the more I feel that the party system is necessary for the working of a democratic and representative system.[16]

No more than TR, however, was Strachey prepared to accept party loyalty as superseding his personal judgment: "one must be prepared to refuse to follow one's party leaders, if not, party becomes a tyrant and not an instrument for effecting political cooperation." [17] Ultimate individual responsibility figured assentially in the Whig temperament both in England and America.[18]

One obsessive fear displayed by Roosevelt and his English correspondents about the successful operation of representative and free governments was the baleful influence of the plutocracy, the materialization of society, and the rise of socialism, these elements woven together in a sinister pattern. As TR commented to Spring Rice,

I am simply unable to understand the value placed by so many people upon great wealth . . . [and] to make myself take the attitude of respect toward the very wealthy men which such an enormous multitude of the people evidently really feel. . . . The very luxurious, grossly material life of the average multimillionaire whom I know does not appeal to me in the least.[19]

Years before Spring Rice had written his own complaint of the "commercial class" [20] and lamented the bad effects of luxury on the race.[21] In America, Roosevelt made a reputation as a foe of the trusts; St. Loe Strachey echoed this view in the editorial columns of the *Spectator,* confiding to TR that "in my opinion the force on which we must chiefly depend to prevent these huge accumulations of capital in single hands is the force of competition. If we can prevent monopolies growing up, the dangers of exaggerated wealth are greatly diminished." [22] More particularly the rich political demogogue constituted a menace to free government, summed up for Roosevelt in the person of William Randolph Hearst. Strachey appreciated the power of such a man and the peril represented to the American republic. "The millionaire demogogue is more dangerous than the demogogue in hobnailed boots," he wrote his friend. "What must make things particularly exasperating for you is to see Hearst caricaturing so vilely your views of the need for proper control of the great and oppressive trusts and combinations." [23] Roosevelt deemed it a "hideous trait" for a man to seek wealth as his sole or highest ambition; and his attitude and that of Strachey toward socialism presupposed their common dread of the unrestrained capitalist.[24]

[11] Roosevelt to Trevelyan, Aug. 18, 1906, *Roosevelt Letters* 5: p. 366.

[12] Roosevelt to Strachey, March 26, 1912, *Roosevelt Letters* 7: p. 531.

[13] Strachey to Roosevelt, June 22, 1908, Roosevelt Papers; Roosevelt to Strachey, March 8, 1901, *Roosevelt Letters* 3: p. 8.

[14] Roosevelt to Bryce, April, 1917, Bryce Papers. (Italics in original.)

[15] Roosevelt to Bryce, Nov. 25, 1898, *Roosevelt Letters* 1: p. 889.

[16] Strachey to Roosevelt, Oct. 1, 1904, Roosevelt Papers.

[17] *Ibid.*

[18] *Ibid.*

[19] Roosevelt to Spring Rice, Sept. 11, 1908, *ibid.*

[20] Spring Rice to Roosevelt, Nov. 3, 1897, *ibid.*

[21] Spring Rice to Roosevelt, May 3, 1897, Spring Rice Papers.

[22] Strachey to Roosevelt, April 23, 1906, Roosevelt Papers.

[23] Strachey to Roosevelt, March 6, 1906, *ibid.*

[24] Roosevelt to Strachey, Sept. 7, 1906, Strachey Papers.

Roosevelt and his friends frequently compared the operation of their respective governments, admiring the strong points of one or the other, and yet remaining on the whole critical. Trevelyan spoke of it in this way:

I suppose each of us is inclined to envy the advantages of a system different from that under which he himself lives. I was much struck by your congratulations upon my being free from the "wearing, distracting and sometimes most ignoble details of parliamentary warfare." They must be wearing and distracting and often ignoble, but upon my word I can hardly believe they are worse than what comes to any American President in the matter of patronage.[25]

The American Commonwealth was simply the most obvious and famous example of mutual admiration. Roosevelt's English correspondence showed that reciprocal esteem was commonplace, a reflex action suggestive of the larger proposition that, after all, the British cabinet system and the American presidential system were only variations of the Anglo-American genius for self-rule.

American executive power came in for any amount of admiration. "What an interesting post is that of Governor of a great American state!" enthused St. Loe Strachey in a letter to TR while the latter was governor of New York. "There is nothing else quite like it in the Anglo-Saxon world. You have more than the power of a King and yet you are in close touch with popular feelings and sentiments."[26] The great prestige of the presidency was lauded in turn. Roosevelt explained a good deal about the office in describing the 1904 presidential campaign to George Otto Trevelyan.

The Presidental campaign is now opening. Apparently I shall be nominated without opposition at the Republican Convention. Whom the Democrates will put up I do not know and of course no one can forecast the results at this time. There is one point of inferiority in our system to yours which has been very little touched on, and this is the way in which the Presidential office tends to put a premium on a man's keeping out of trouble rather than upon his accomplishing results. If a man has a very decided character, has a strongly accentuated career, it is normally the case of course that he makes ardent friends and bitter enemies; and unfortunately human nature is such that more enemies will leave their party because of enmity at its head than friends will come in from the opposite party because they think well of the same head. In consequence the dark horse, the neutral tinted individual, is very apt to win against the man of pronounced views and active life. Now all this does not apply to the same extent with your Prime Minister.[27]

Having spoken so earnestly to Trevelyan of the ambiguities of the presidential campaign, when the results were in the Englishman wrote jubilantly to Roosevelt: "I was relieved as well as rejoiced by the great news," adding, "I am deeply anxious that a ruler, who so

read his duty should continue where he was for the benefit of his country and the world."[28] In a further reflection on the 1904 election Roosevelt again made comparison between the American and the English systems of government.

Although the canvass naturally caused me at times a good deal of worry, I did not have too much work to do. Each Nation has its conventions. Whereas the Prime Minister is expected to take the stump on his own behalf, it is regarded as improper for a President to do so. This is the kind of custom which could be disregarded in a great emergency, but which is never wise or politic to disregard for insufficient reason. In the same way it has become one of our customs, with even more than conventional force, that no President is to have a third term; whereas in England the longer the Prime Minister serves, the more he is esteemed as having been true to his party.[29]

Shortly after his inauguration in 1905 the president wrote again to Trevelyan on the nature of the executive office, referring to "the tremendous responsibilities of my position." He pointed out that his power, great as it was, did not obviate the possibility of defeat. "Life is a long campaign where every victory merely leaves the ground free for another battle, and sooner or later the defeat comes to every man, unless death forestalls it."[30] Trevelyan was more optimistic:

I know you have your share of troubles and annoyances which beset every ruler who is working for the country, and not for himself; "but I am glad to think that you can choose your own time for making communications to the public, and are not bound to engage in controversy with every coxcomb in a white tie and evening clothes who comes to worry a Minister who has been working continuously since he rose from a bad night's sleep.[31]

Their individual political experiences had bred in both Roosevelt and Trevelyan a realism which occasionally could shade into cynicism.

Such discussions occasioned one or the other of the friends to indulge in historical rumination. The president had expressed his worry to Trevelyan that the 1906 congressional elections might go against the Republican party and thus he was concerned over the prospect of an uncooperative legislature in the months to follow.[32] Trevelyan's response reminds one of how much the lessons of history colored comments on the present. He wrote at some length.

Whatever may have been the wisdom, or otherwise, of changing the legislature during the not overlong tenure of the Executive, as far as *theory* goes, it is in *practice* deplorable, unless the Executive needs checking, watching, or even replacing. Under the French Constitution of 1795 the Directory found itself periodically face to face with a

25 Trevelyan to Roosevelt, May 13, 1905, Bishop, 1920: 2: p. 149.
26 Strachey to Roosevelt, Feb. 1, 1900, Roosevelt Papers.
27 Roosevelt to Trevelyan, May 28, 1904, *Roosevelt Letters* 5: p. 806.

28 Trevelyan to Roosevelt, Nov. 10, 1904, Roosevelt Papers.
29 Roosevelt to Trevelyan, Nov. 24. 1904, *Roosevelt Letters* 4: p. 1132.
30 Roosevelt to Trevelyan, March 9, 1905, *ibid.* 4: p. 1132.
31 Trevelyan to Roosevelt, March 30, 1905, Bishop, 1920: 2: pp. 147–148.
32 Roosevelt to Trevelyan, Aug. 18, 1906, *Roosevelt Letters* 5: p. 365.

fresh installment of political opponents in the Chamber. They solved the difficulty, after the simple fashion of those days, by a regularly recurring coup d'etat, until Bonaparte settled it finally by sending both the Directory and the Chamber to the right-about. I earnestly hope that you will have a more sympathetic Legislature to cooperate with you![33]

All of which the president probably found of interest, but of little consolation.

The office of president being unique the figure of an ex-president was necessarily so. Strachey and Roosevelt discussed the "problem" of ex-presidents, and if they were unable to agree on any solution, their common concern was typical of that sense of kinship featuring these political exchanges. Strachey had written in the *Spectator* that an ex-president ought to be retained by the government and kept on its payroll, both to take advantage of his experience and to save him from the possibility of financial difficulties embarrassing to the nation. Roosevelt objected, having his own future in mind. "I am not sure that I altogether agree with your article," he argued.

When people have spoken to me as to what America should do with its ex-presidents, I have always answered that there was one ex-president as to whom they need not concern themselves in the least, because I would do for myself. It would be to me personally an unpleasant thing to be pensioned and given some honorary position. I emphatically do not desire to clutch at the fringe of departing greatness. Indeed there is something rather attractive, something in a way living up to the proper democratic ideal in having a president go out of office just as I shall go, and become absolutely without reservation a private man.[34]

Unconvinced by this bit of selfconscious preaching, Strachey reacted with a mixture of admiration and obstinacy.

. . . If you were the only man who will ever become an ex-president, I should be quite content that things remain as they are. . . . What we have to consider, however, is not you but the normal man. Personally I am not afraid of a normal man doing anything wrong, but I do think that after the Republic has made him what he is by having endowed him with the powers and responsibilities of a president, it is better that the public should retain his services for the rest of his life. There will be plenty of work for him to do, and the State, by paying him, obtains the right to put him beyond the temptation to do work which is not suitable for a man who has held such vast responsibilities. . . .[35]

Strachey's argument showed that his chief concern was the good name of the American Republic, a concern not entirely devoid of sentiment.

On occasion the American Senate, because of its treaty-making role, affected Anglo-American relations, with the result that British politicians looked upon the upper house of the Congress with a blend of incomprehension and suspicion. Strachey for one voiced his doubts about the Senate to President Roosevelt.

I wish the Senate had, like our House of Lords, no power over money bills. Entire power over the purse would so enormously raise the status of the Lower House. . . . To tell the truth, what concerns me is the appearance of a want of sense of responsibility in the Senate despite its vast powers.[36]

The president thought his friend had an incomplete knowledge of the Senate and sought to explain something more of it to him. "What you say about the Senate is entirely true. It is a very powerful body with an illustrious history, and life in it is easy . . . the esprit de corps of the Senate is high . . . [it] has an immense capacity for resistance." Then TR changed the pace of his argument.

Let me say at the same time, however, that the Senate has many admirable parts. There are few positions better worth filling than that of Senator . . . men like Lodge and many others I could mention spend their time as hard as they know how for the public good. The extreme conservatism of the Senate has very distinct uses in as purely democratic a country as ours. . . . In domestic politics Congress in the long run is apt to do what is right. It is in foreign affairs and in matters of the army and the navy that we are apt to have the most difficulty, because these are subjects to which the average American citizen does not take the trouble to think carefully or deeply.[37]

Just as each nation had its own conventions, so also each nation had its peculiar institutions and powers appropriate to the history and needs of that nation. The friendly, informed disagreements which sometimes arose between Roosevelt and his correspondents enabled them to perceive the existing distinctions between their governmental forms while deepening an awareness of the basic similarities between the two peoples.

This same lesson was manifested in the Roosevelt-Lee discussion of the differences in electoral methods between the two nations. Writing after the General Election of 1910 in Great Britain, Lee observed: "Personally I wish we had the American system of all elections on one day as I am sure it gets a truer picture of the verdict by it. Here a large section of the electors wait until the earlier results show which way the tide is moving and then vote so as to be on the winning side."[38] Up to a point, Roosevelt concurred with him. "I entirely agree with you that the American system of having all elections on the same day tends to get a better verdict. Here, however, there is the exception of having Maine and Vermont vote first, and they always have a real effect on the after vote."[39] As part of this same political dialogue, Lee spoke of his fear

[33] Trevelyan to Roosevelt, Aug. 28, 1906, Roosevelt Papers.
[34] Roosevelt to Strachey, Nov. 28, 1908, *Roosevelt Letters* 6: p. 1388.
[35] Strachey to Roosevelt, Dec. 19, 1908, Roosevelt Papers.

[36] Strachey to Roosevelt, Jan. 29, 1906, Strachey Papers.
[37] Roosevelt to Strachey, Feb. 12, 1906, *Roosevelt Letters* 6: pp. 150–151.
[38] Lee to Roosevelt, Jan. 9, 1911, Roosevelt Papers.
[39] Roosevelt to Lee, Feb. 2, 1911, Lee Papers. See also Roosevelt to Lee, Jan. 5, 1907, *ibid.*

that the Liberal government, supported by Irish and Labor votes, was about to scrap "the whole edifice [of the English constitution] and erect an omnipotent House of Commons on the ruins." [40] Surveying the American scene, Roosevelt's reply was in an equally uneasy vein.

The thing that makes me alarmed here is the growth of tendencies which will have their ultimate and very evil effects not immediately but a generation or two hence. We have difficult problems to face even in politics, for we must not see this grow into a government of plutocracy, nor yet into a government by mob.[41]

As thoughtful men, Lee, Roosevelt, and the others were likely to look beyond the machinery of politics to the substance of events and what meaning it held for the future of the two countries.

The small talk of Roosevelt and his friends, spanning a quarter of a century, was both a fund of political opinion and a persuasive indication of the common outlook intrinsic to the developing rapprochement. In one or two instances at least this kind of intimate conversation via letters displayed insights into govermental problems attributable only to more acute observers of the political universe. St. Loe Strachey's discussion of law and order in the United States was a good example. As almost always, Strachey was worried about the good name and the good practice of law in America; he was specifically concerned about "lynch law" which he viewed as part of a dangerous tendency toward ready homicide. Roosevelt himself was a firm and outspoken opponent of lynching, calling it "one of the greatest blots in American civilization." In his annual message to the Congress in 1904 he referred to the problem indirectly, and in his 1906 message characterized lynch law as a "loosening of the bands of civilization." The condition of lawlessness in the United States, "the terrible growth of murder and homicide" troubled Strachey so much that he took up the problem in the pages of the *Spectator* in 1904. And writing privately to TR he made a number of shrewd observations.

I confess that to me, as an outsider, it seems hardly possible that you [as President] can do anything effective owing to the States rights, but though my reason tells me that you are bound hand and foot I admit that I feel instinctively that somehow you will manage to do something big and practical. How I wish the fathers of the Constitution had made murder and all great felonies federal matters! Then you could have had a federal police force through-out the country. I may be utterly wrong, but it always seems to me that what is wanted in America, under modern conditions, is not more or better law, or more or better justice, but more and better police. You have plenty of cure, but not enough prevention and there is nothing truer than that "prevention is better than cure." [42]

After Roosevelt's election in 1904, he announced that he would not seek another term of office in 1908. This was a curious decision if only because it was made so far in advance by a man who enjoyed the uses of political power. The decision involved the third term tradition as well as other aspects of American politics and it came in for some lively discussion between Roosevelt and George O. Trevelyan. In June of 1908, shortly after the Republican convention had nominated William Howard Taft for president, TR wrote a long letter to his friend. Touching on many items of mutual interest, it contained an arresting explanation of the decision not to run. It had been a "curious contest" in 1908, the president told Trevelyan, "for I have had to fight tooth and nail against being nominated myself." Roosevelt contended that when he had decided not to run he had "acted on a carefully thought-out and considered theory." But, he confided, "the developments of the last year or two have been so out of the common that at times I have felt a little uncomfortable as to whether my announced decision had been wise," adding grimly, "but I think it was wise; and now I want to give you my reasons in full." These reasons included: the precedent set by Washington, the wisdom of great power held by one man only for short times, the expectation in a republic that the public good supersedes personal ambition, TR's personal desire for history to place him in the Washington-Lincoln tradition, his fear that should he seek another term and win it the multitude of voters would "have a feeling of disappointment" because he deemed it proper to hold the presidency longer than Washington.[43] Genuinely touched by the candor of Roosevelt's letter, Trevelyan wrote in response:

Your letter was deeply interesting and it convinced me. It is impossible to overestimate the value of such an act of deliberate and reasoned consistency, maintained under pressure so severe and constant, and amidst so many and so fervent appeals to high motive of public duty, and from so great a mass of affection and confidence. I immensely appreciate the contrast between your unshrinking vindication of the extreme authority of the Executive power and your inflexible determination to lay down that power at the exact moment you had fixed in your own mind and announced it to the world. . . . Mr. Gladstone (so I have come to believe) committed a grave mistake in 1880, when he resumed the leadership he had solemnly renounced. . . . No good and much harm came from his course of action.[44]

After Taft's election Trevelyan again wrote to say, "you have carried through a most abstruse and delicate task in your attitude towards the recent Presidential election," a final tribute to Theodore Roosevelt's political restraint.[45]

Among a host of other topics which produced perceptive commentary were the use of a title for the president, Taft's nomination in 1908, the drift of Progressivism

[40] Lee to Roosevelt, Jan. 9, 1911, Roosevelt Papers.
[41] Roosevelt to Lee, Feb. 2, 1911, Lee Papers.
[42] Strachey to Roosevelt, Dec. 29, 1904, Roosevelt Papers.

[43] Roosevelt to Trevelyan, June 19, 1908, *Roosevelt Letters* 6: pp. 1085–1087.
[44] Trevelyan to Roosevelt, June 30, 1908, Roosevelt Papers.
[45] Trevelyan to Roosevelt, Nov. 17, 1908, *ibid.*

under Taft, the struggle between the Liberal party and the House of Lords in England, and the attempt on TR's life in the presidential campaign of 1912. Attention to incidental matters, like the use of a title for the president, in the correspondence adds to an understanding both of the friendships themselves and the intellectual commitment that was part of the rise of Anglo-American accord. Trevelyan once asked TR about a title for the president. "I do not know whether I am correct in addressing you as 'Excellency,' but I like doing it because of Charles Lee's objection to that title for Washington."[46] Roosevelt replied seriously and at some length.

I would rather not be called Excellency and this partly because the title does not belong to me and partly from vanity! The President of the United States ought to have no title; and if he did have a title it ought be a bigger one. Whenever an important prince comes here he is apt to bring a shoal of "Excellencies" in his train. Just as I should object to having the simple dignity of the White House changed for such attractions as might lie in a second rate palace, so I feel that the President of a great democratic republic should have no title that would not be either too much or too little. Let him be called the President, and nothing more.[47]

St. Loe Strachey thought it "plain as a pikestaff" that TR "had carried Mr. Taft at the Convention" and sent Roosevelt his congratulations,[48] while Roosevelt told Arthur Lee in September, 1908, that he thought Taft would be elected "perhaps not by quite such a popular majority as mine but by substantially the same electoral vote."[49] Taft's irresolute leadership as president was also discussed by Roosevelt and Lee. When the ex-president returned home after his Afro-European tour he discovered a Republican party that was seriously divided between Taft and Progressivism. He kept in touch with Lee throughout the late summer of 1910. In July he described his position as one of "inconceivable difficulty," as he was still anxious to support Taft and maintain party unity.[50] By August he admitted that politics were "worse rather than better. Taft, who is such an admirable fellow, has shown himself such an utterly commonplace leader."[51] In September the situation, in TR's judgment, had become "anything but pleasant" as he faced the disagreeable prospect of having to struggle once more for control of the New York State machine.[52] Lee followed these reports with "enormous interest," reading the American newspapers "diligently." He sympathized with Roosevelt about the "increasing inability of the President to cope with

various elements of the situation," offering the estimate that Taft had no prospects for re-election in 1912. "I fear the day has gone by when it is sufficient qualification for the President to have 'taught school' or have been good to one's mother," he added sardonically. As Lee read the signs, events were conspiring to bring his friend, "however unwillingly—into the position where you will have to choose between the complete overthrow of your Party or acceptance of Leadership."[53] Lee continued to keep a close watch on the 1910 campaign, at one moment confessing that he did not understand American politics well enough to appreciate the total situation, but that his concern for America and her welfare caused him to await the outcome with apprehension.[54]

Conversely Roosevelt, through his friends' letters, savored the struggle in England to reduce the power of the House of Lords, and so further democratize the British system of government. He got both conservative and liberal points of view. Strachey, for example, did not like the Trades Disputes Bill of 1906.

It seems to me quite contrary to all true principles of Anglo-Saxon polity to create a privileged caste, but that is what we are doing. Whether the House of Lords will have the pluck to strike out the clauses conferring caste privileges upon the Trades Unions remains to be seen, but I am a little afraid whether they may not say that this is a case in which they must bow to the will of the House of Commons.[55]

Trevelyan summed up the larger problem involved somewhat differently: a strong Liberal Government and the House of Lords "cannot co-exist," he held. For Trevelyan, a reduction of the veto power of the Lords was "the dominating issue in politics." He was sure, furthermore, that Roosevelt was sympathetic to this stand. "If you had a House of Lords, I should dearly love to hear the speeches you would make about it."[56] As the Liberal vs. Lords issue built up to a climax, Trevelyan was more and more anxious to represent his views as cogently as possible, at a time when Roosevelt's own radicalism was becoming pronounced. Sending Christmas greetings in 1910, Sir George called the political issue in England at that time "very simple, clear and impossible to muddle or obscure. Ever since the Great Reform Bill the House of Lords have rejected many Liberal measures and no Tory measures whatever."[57] As the fight wore on Arthur Lee gave TR his version of things. "In your conservative country I notice that a convulsion of sudden passes over the entire continent if any individual hints that there may be a surface crack in one of the pillars of the Constitution. Here," he lamented, "we are light-heartedly going to scrap the whole edifice. . . . I will

[46] Trevelyan to Roosevelt, March 30, 1905, Bishop, 1920: 2: p. 147.
[47] Roosevelt to Trevelyan, May 13, 1905, *Roosevelt Letters* 6: p. 1173.
[48] Strachey to Roosevelt, June 22, 1908, Roosevelt Papers.
[49] Roosevelt to Lee, Sept. 2, 1908, *Roosevelt Letters* 6: p. 1205.
[50] Roosevelt to Lee, Aug. 12, 1910, *ibid.* 7: p. 103.
[51] *Ibid.* 7: p. 112.
[52] Roosevelt to Lee, Sept. 16, 1910, *ibid.* 7: p. 129.

[53] Lee to Roosevelt, Sept. 7, 1910, Roosevelt Papers.
[54] Lee to Roosevelt, Nov. 1, 1910, *ibid.*
[55] Strachey to Roosevelt, Nov. 6, 1906, *ibid.*
[56] Trevelyan to Roosevelt, Dec. 15, 1906, *ibid.*
[57] Trevelyan to Roosevelt, Dec. 16, 1910, *ibid.*

not attempt to forecast where all this is going to lead us, but for the immediate future we have got to face the most savage fight in Parliament. . . . I feel *murderous* and if you should hear of my developing homicidal tendencies you must not be surprised." [58] Roosevelt's reaction to the Liberal vs. Lords controversy and his friends' varying estimates of it was cautious but unambiguous. To Trevelyan he crisply noted: "looking at it as an outsider . . . you are doing pretty well." [59] He wrote to Arthur Lee at greater length, probably because he disagreed with him.

I want to get your views as to just exactly what the situation is now in England—I do not mean temporarily, but permanently—with the power of the House of Lords so completely altered. Do you think that if the Conservatives come in they will endeavor to reconfer upon the House of Lords their former power? It is none of my affair, and I know nothing of the subject, but I should think such an effort would be unwise. . . . My feeling about the House of Lords is a good deal like my feeling about our judiciary in regard to popular movements; that it is all right for them to have power to stop hasty ill-considered action and make people think, but when once the people have thought the subject out, the people must have the power to carry their determination into effect.[60]

Roosevelt later explained that despite his Progressive frame of mind, which grew to a climax in 1912, they must remain political and personal friends. Lee returned an understanding letter, to which Roosevelt replied: "I had been a little bit uncomfortable for fear you might not sympathize with it [Progressivism] because it really *is* a democratic movement. But as you know, I have always believed that wise progressivism and wise conservatism go hand in hand." [61] In such discussions though the correspondents might defer to one another as "outsiders," "who knew nothing of such matters," the penetration of their observations argued otherwise. And in these conversations, though disagreements sometimes occurred, the friendships suffered no ill effects.

The attempt on Theodore Roosevelt's life during the 1912 presidential campaign caused a great deal of concern on the part of his English friends and brought forth some noteworthy comment on the problem of assassinations in public life. To George O. Trevelyan Roosevelt wrote philosophically.

It is just as you say; prominence in public life inevitably means that creatures of morbid or semi-criminal type are incited thereby to murderous assault. But, my dear Sir George, I must say I have never understood public men who get nervous about assassination. For the last eleven years I have of course thoroughly understood that I might at any time be shot, and probably would be shot sometime. I think I have come off uncommonly well. But what I can't understand is any serious-minded public man not being absorbed in the great and vital questions with which he has to deal as to exclude thoughts of assassination. I do not think this is a question of the major interest driving out the minor interest. . . . As I say, it is not a question of courage; it is a question of perspective, or proper proportion. . . . I have never felt that public men who were shot whether they were killed or not, were entitled to any special sympathy. . . .[62]

Strachey, a man of different temper, got a blunt appraisal:

Just one word about the mad man who shot me. He was not really a mad-man at all. . . . I very seriously question if he has a more unsound brain than Senator La Follette or Eugene Debs. . . . He had quite enough sense to avoid shooting me in any Southern State, where he would have been lynched, and he waited until he got into a state where there was no death penalty. I have not the slightest feeling against him; I have a very strong feeling against the people, who, by their ceaseless and intemperate abuse, excited him to action and against the mushy people who would excuse him and all other criminals once the crime had been committed.[63]

Strachey replied:

I was delighted to find such proof of your recovery to vigorous health again as your letter of December 16th. All you tell me about the mad-man who shot you is very curious and interesting. I hold that you are absolutely right in putting the blame where it ought to be put, that is, upon the men who indirectly but nonetheless surely excited the crime by representing you as a "fiend of Hell." [64]

Relieved that his friend was alive, Strachey was little disposed to argue Roosevelt's acid judgment.

The scope and tone of political discussion between Theodore Roosevelt and his English correspondents displayed "a sympathy of comprehension," enabling them to appreciate the political world they shared. To St. Loe Strachey the reasons were plain. "The differences of our systems [of government] are superficial, the likenesses fundamental. We speak the same language, recognize the same common law principles in our law and administration, and are inspired by the same political and moral ideals." [65] All the Roosevelt circle subscribed to much the same testament, so well and so pointedly summarized in TR's remark to Arthur Lee that the Anglo-Americans were "the only two really free great peoples."

Roosevelt and his friends were deeply conscious of History. The closely related political systems of the two countries were the result of a long historical buildup, just as they saw Anglo-American hegemony in the world as the working out of a complex historical process. Roosevelt was especially aware that the conquest of the American frontier represented an extension of the

---

[58] Lee to Roosevelt, Jan. 9, 1911, *ibid.* (Italcis in original.)

[59] Roosevelt to Trevelyan, July 24, 1911, *Roosevelt Letters* 7: p. 313.

[60] Roosevelt to Lee, Aug. 22, 1911, *ibid.* 7: p. 337.

[61] Roosevelt to Lee, Aug. 14, 1912, *ibid.* 7: p. 597. (Italics in original.)

[62] Roosevelt to Trevelyan, Oct. 29, 1912, Bishop, 1920: 2: p. 175.

[63] Roosevelt to Strachey, Dec. 16, 1912, *Roosevelt Letters* 7: pp. 676-677.

[64] Strachey to Roosevelt, Jan. 23, 1913, Roosevelt Papers.

[65] Strachey to Roosevelt, March 10, 1906, Strachey Papers.

larger movement of "men speaking English" across the world begun centuries before. At the opening of his most ambitious historical work, *The Winning of the West,* he laid down what must be considered one of his fundamental contentions of modern history.

During the past three centuries the spread of English speaking peoples over the world's waste spaces has been not only the most striking feature in the world's history, but also the events of all others most far-reaching in its effects and its importance.[66]

This theme was woven throughout the description and analysis which followed. Among others to whom TR sent copies of his book was fellow-historian, James Bryce. Bryce favored Roosevelt's interpretation and in thanking him for his interest Roosevelt again spoke of the frontier conquest as the "mighty epoch in the career of the mighty English race." [67] TR elaborated his views to Spring Rice.

To you India seems larger than Australia. In the life history of the English speaking people I think it will show very much smaller. The Australians are building up a great commonwealth, the very existence of which, like the existence of the United States, means an alteration in the balance of power of the world and goes a long way towards insuring the supremacy of men who speak our tongue and have our ideals of social, political, and religious freedom and morality.[68]

What, in fact, were the prospects for the continued world position of the Anglo-American peoples?

The British Empire appeared to have reached its peak by 1900 and the American frontier had closed. A high concern of both nations was the future of the "world movement" of the Eiglish-speaking peoples. Was it to maintain itself, or to succumb to more powerful historical forces? To men such as Roosevelt and his friends, who proposed to be masters of events, there was no more serious proposition. The rise of the new Germany, the unfathomable future direction of the Russian State, and the chaotic conditions in China were all cause for concern. Spring Rice, constantly abroad and in touch with foreign situations and the foreign mind, wrote Roosevelt of the German and the Russian threat. Even before the outbreak of the Spanish War he advised his friend of German hostility to the United States. "To begin with," he commented from Berlin, "there is the feud here that every official German has with America, which is regarded as a huge machine for teaching Germans English and making them Republican." The future was ominous, according to Spring Rice.

Germany increases by 650,000 persons every year. The productive power of the country has reached its limits and every year Germany must acquire more of her supplies from abroad. The drive for possessions was thus ordained. In

Spring Rice's judgment Germany's overseas expansion would be influenced by certain internal conditions which he was anxious to explain. To become a great colonial power required a large navy, a large navy in turn hurt the agricultural interests in Germany and the army, just as it served the advantage of the commercial and industrial classes. This dichotomy was really at the foot of the constant political struggles which are taking place here. The Emperor, who is burning to have a big navy and has to pay for it, can not consent to anything that would cripple the manufacturing and commercial interests in the country. On the other hand he is bound by sympathy and tradition to the class which has fought for his family in countless wars and which has really made Germany possible. The question is a natural one, and one can sympathize with both sides.[69]

Spring Rice had said by inference that should the Kaiser come into possession of both a powerful navy and army a German threat to the Anglo-American nations could materialize. By 1900 St. Loe Strachey was probing the same area of misgiving.

I have it most strongly in my mind that Germany is building her Great Fleet in order to defy the Monroe Doctrine. . . . Not to attack you of course. They would never dream of that, but in order to say: "thank you, we can manage our own affairs," when she steps in to protect German property in Southern Brazil.[70]

In writing his English friends, TR took a look at the situation from the German corner.

If I were a German I should want the German race to expand. I should be glad to see it begin to expand in the only two places left for ethnic, as distinguished from the political expansion of the European peoples, that is, in South Africa and in the temperate parts of South America. Therefore as a German I should be delighted to upset the English in South Africa and to defy the Americans and their Monroe Doctrine in South America. As an Englishmen I would seize the first opportunity to crush the German Navy and the German commercial marine out of existence, and take possession of both the German possessions and Portuguese possessions in South Africa, leaving the Boers absolutely isolated. As an American I should advocate—and as a matter of fact do advocate—keeping our Navy at a pitch that will enable us to interfere promptly if Germany ventures to touch a foot of American soil. I would not go into the abstract rights or wrongs of it; I would simply say that we did not intend to have Germans on this continent . . . if Germany intended to extend her empire here she would have to whip us first.

Reflective of his historical orientation, Roosevelt then attempted to estimate the existing international situation in terms of the politics of antiquity. He referred specifically to the Russo-German rivalry and the possibility of a *drang nach Osten.*

Of course, if Germany has adopted the views of some of the Greek states, . . . [as] the Achaean League adopted toward Rome after the second Punic War, I have nothing more to say. These Greek states made up their mind that Rome had the future. . . . If Germany feels this way toward Russia, well and good. . . . If the Kaiser were a Frederick the Great or a Gustavus Adolphus, if he were a Cromwell, a

[66] Roosevelt, *The Winning of the West. Works* 10: p. 3.

[67] Roosevelt to Bryce, March 13, 1891, Bryce Papers.

[68] Roosevelt to Spring Rice, Aug. 11, 1899, *Roosevelt Letters* 2: p. 1052.

[69] Spring Rice to Roosevelt, Nov. 3, 1897, Spring Rice Papers.

[70] Strachey to Roosevelt, Jan. 15, 1900, Roosevelt Papers.

Pitt, or like Andrew Jackson, had the "instinct for the jugular," he would recognize his real foe and strike savagely at the point where danger threatens.[71]

Writing to Arthur Lee about the same time on the same matter, Roosevelt assumed an unmistakably pro-British attitude. "If the powers of continental Europe menace your people, I believe and certainly hope this country will promptly give them notice: 'hand off!' But I think your navy will guarantee you against interference." A postscript to this letter re-enforced his assertion. "Col. Shaw, the Commander of the Grand Army of the Republic, has been in; I read him what I had written you as regards our attitude in the event of the Continent menacing England, and he said: 'Tell him I agree with every word; we're for England'." [72] What Roosevelt and his friends feared was more than military aggression, they foresaw the possible submergence of their polities and their culture. "Liberalism . . . is by far the most dangerous system of all in the eyes of the ruling classes here," Spring Rice wrote from Berlin in 1897, by way of advising TR of the official German view of emigration. "Men can't catch the mange. Germans can't catch Russian absolutism or South American anarchy. But they are extremely liable to catch Anglo-Saxon Liberalism, especially when imported by their own return emigrants." [73] Spring Rice went on to expound his version of the cultural differences between the Anglo-Americans and the Germans with great force. The central European system of government put the free English peoples at a disadvantage, he thought. In any struggle the Germans would profit greatly from their autocratic and continuous government while England and America could expect the corresponding disadvantage that fickle public opinion brings to representative rule. The press, he continued, had all too often sown bad seed between England and America, instead of stressing cultural similarities.

How can one bring angry people together? . . . A genuine burst of public sympathy and admiration ought to make it possible, should the object be a great one, to work cordially together. . . . [It] would mean possibly that our race and civilization are safe. . . . I don't care for black millions and red maps; what I do care for, which I learned from you, is a brave, manly, honest people; the people who speak English throughout the world.

Whether Germany would succeed in extending herself outside the limits of central Europe, thereby enlarging the threat of her distinctive culture, Spring Rice believed would be decided by the middle of the twentieth century. The Anglo-Americans faced a very severe testing time ahead.[74]

Russia also constituted a peril. Spring Rice's estimate of the Russian challenge was chilling indeed. One thing that troubled him, he told Roosevelt, was Russia's self-sufficiency. "She is practically invulnerable to attack. She is growing and has room to grow. She is also gradually acquiring command over the war-like races with whom she can carry out a sort of military assimilation, for which her constitution is specially fitted." Spring Rice insisted on seeing Russia in a large historical focus. "If America disintegrates, as some Americans maintain is possible,—or if it goes mad like Spanish America—the future of the world is not improbably in the hands of the Slavs." [75] The Russians both amazed and frightened Spring Rice.

I hear them talk, and think of a Hun or a Goth at the court of Constantine. They like and yet despise our civilization and firmly believe that it will be theirs in time. They watch the fruits of civilization growing, intending when they are ripe, to come and take them. . . . They contrast Siberia with North America and say how evident it is that the Russians and only they are the pioneers of a true civilization. . . . They don't care for the inventions of our race except as a means to use. They will develop their own form of Government, literature, and art. They despise all of us but none perhaps as much as the Americans, who have, they say, the faults of the old world without its *agrements*.[76]

The intrinsic differences between the Russians and the Anglo-Americans were evidently uppermost in the mind of Spring Rice. He was also worried about Russian dominance in China and what that would imply for the English-speaking race should it come about.[77]

Roosevelt freely acknowledged the Russian menace. "Indeed Russia is a problem very appalling," he responded to Spring Rice.

All other nations of European blood, if they develop at all, seem inclined to develop on much the same lines; but Russia seems bound to develop in her own way, and on lines that run directly counter to what we are accustomed to consider as progress. If she ever does take possession of Northern China and drill the North Chinese to serve as her Army, she will indeed be a formidable power. . . . The growth of the great Russian state in Siberia is portentous, but it is stranger still nowadays to see the rulers of the nation deliberately keeping it under a despotism, deliberately setting their faces against any increase of the share of the people in government.[78]

Roosevelt discounted the fact that Russia and America had maintained friendly relations in the past, though unlike Spring Rice he recognized no pressing threat. So much of the Anglo-American view of past history and future developments appeared in the passages of one of Theodore Roosevelt's letters responding to Spring Rice's observations on the state of the world at the

71 Roosevelt to Spring Rice, Aug. 13, 1897, *Roosevelt Letters* 1: p. 645.
72 Roosevelt to Lee, Dec. 19, 1899, Lee Papers.
73 Spring Rice to Roosevelt, Nov. 15, 1898, Gwynn, 1920: 1: pp. 269–270.
74 Spring Rice to Roosevelt, Sept. 14, 1896, *ibid.* 1: p. 211.

75 *Ibid.*
76 Spring Rice to Roosevelt, Aug. 1, 1897, *ibid.* 1: pp. 228–229. (Italics in original.)
77 Spring Rice to Roosevelt, July 18, 1898, *ibid.* 1: p. 210.
78 Roosevelt to Spring Rice, Aug. 5, 1896, *Roosevelt Letters* 1: p. 555; see also Roosevelt to Spring Rice, March 19, 1904, Gwynn, 1929: 1: p. 397.

close of the nineteenth century that it merits extensive quotation.

Now about the Russians. Russia and the United States are friendly but Russians and Americans in their individual capacity have nothing whatever in common. That they despise Americans in a way is doubtless true. I rather doubt if they despise Europeans. . . . As for our attitude toward them, I don't quite take your view, which seems to be, after all, merely a reflection of theirs. Evidently you look upon them as they think they should be looked upon—that is as huge, powerful barbarians, cynically confident that they will in the end inherit the fruits of our civilization, firmly believing that the future belongs to them . . . despising as effete all of Europe and especially America. I look upon them as a people to whom we can give points, and a beating; a people with a great future, as we have; but a people with poisons working in it, as other poisons, of similar character on the whole, work in us.
Well, there is a certain justification for your view, but the people who have least to fear from Russians are the people who can speak English. They may overrun the continent of Europe, but they cannot touch your people or mine, unless perhaps in India. There is no such difference between them and us as there was between the Goths and the Byzantines; it will be many a long year before we lose our capacity to lay out those Goths. They are below the Germans just as the Germans are below us; the space between the German and the Russian may be greater than that between the Englishman and the German, but that is all. . . . If Russia chooses to develop purely on her own line and to resist the growth of liberalism, then she may put off the day of reckoning; but she can not ultimately avert it, and instead of occasionally having to go through what Kansas has gone through with the populists she will sometime experience a real terror which will make the French Revolution pale. Meanwhile one curious fact is forgotten: The English-speaking people have never gone back before the Slav, and the Slav has never gone back before them save once: . . . the American—the man of effete English speaking races—has driven the Slav from the eastern coast of the North Pacific.[79]

Clearly Roosevelt's estimate of the Russians was less pessimistic than that of Spring Rice but soberly realistic nonetheless.

Fear of Russia became nothing less than an obsession for Spring Rice as evidenced in his letters to TR. In 1899 he again stressed the differences between the Russians and his own peoples. "What strikes me most about the Russians is her contempt for Europe, France included. 'We are not Europeans, we are Russians!'" He contrasted the growth of Russia with that of the Anglo-Americans, asking: "Are we on the going down side of the wheel? I should like to see England and America friends, because I think they support together the best that history shows."[80] Roosevelt listened sympathetically but he was not fully discouraged.

I understand all that you feel about Russia. . . . As I said in one of my former letters you feel as the Greeks at the time of Demosthenes felt toward Macedonia. That there is ground for your apprehension I fully admit but,

historically analogies must always be carefully guarded, and I am not at all sure that the Macedonian analogy will hold.

Roosevelt insisted that their race, the Anglo-American, was not effete, "not the slightest symptom of its decadence as yet, whether in military, administrative or in business and social matters. I should not envy the Russian General who clashed with Kitchener."[81] Spring Rice remained unconvinced and uneasy. Russian conquest "is not so much a mechanistic as an organic conquest," he reminded his friend.[82]

By 1905 both St. Loe Strachey and Spring Rice were writing the president about the future of Russia and by implication the Russian posture vis-à-vis the Anglo-American nations. In a letter to Edith Carow Roosevelt sent from St. Petersburg in March, 1905, Spring Rice exuded pessimism, particularly because of the cultural disparity between Slav and Anglo-Saxon. "We have read the Manifesto of the Czar in which he tells us he is determined to maintain the contrary principles to free government and to take his stand on that. We shall see with what results. . . . This manifesto was his own heart-felt expression of conviction."[83] Strachey in contrast was somewhat more sanguine, putting forth the hope that "Russia will move, no matter how sluggishly and haltingly, forward on the path of self-government," though he admitted that she "can not take her place in the twentieth century if she adheres to the spirit and methods of Ivan the Terrible."[84] Despite the formation of the Triple Entente in 1907, which lessened to a degree the menace of Russia to the British dominated areas of the world, the specter would not entirely dissolve. Strachey wrote to Roosevelt in 1913:

I do not know what your feeling about the Slavs is from experience on the other side of the Atlantic. In my opinion we in Europe are going to have to think a great deal more about the Slavs in the next few years than we have ever thought before. They will, before long, either upset and destroy or else profoundly modify the Austrian Empire. But if they modify it I do not believe that the German elements will remain.

He added, "however this is all speculation and perhaps fruitless speculation."[85] The seeds of distrust, many of which Spring Rice had sown in the 1890's, if they had not come to full growth, did represent an element of concern on the part of Roosevelt and his friends down to the eve of the 1914 war.

The Roosevelt coterie also brought a sense of history to a consideration of what Captain Mahan spoke of as "the problem of Asia." China was all but helpless to defend herself against a continuing commercial conquest

[79] Roosevelt to Spring Rice, Aug. 13, 1897, *Roosevelt Letters* 1: pp. 646–647.
[80] Spring Rice to Roosevelt, Jan. 27, 1899, Spring Rice Papers.

[81] Roosevelt to Spring Rice, Aug. 11, 1899, *Roosevelt Letters* 1: p. 1051.
[82] Spring Rice to Roosevelt, Jan. 3, 1901, Roosevelt Papers.
[83] Spring Rice to Edith Carow Roosevelt, March 13, 1905, *ibid.*
[84] Strachey to Roosevelt, Sept. 11, 1905, Strachey Papers.
[85] Strachey to Roosevelt, Jan. 23, 1911, *ibid.*

by the Western capitalist Powers, of which Great Britain was in the front rank, nor was she able to hold off a political conquest should it come at the hands of Russia or Japan. When revolution broke out in China in 1900, TR saw such a turn of events as inimical to the English speaking nations. "I agree with every word you say," he wrote Arthur Lee, "as to the need of every decent man working steadily to bring about an ever increasing sympathy and understanding between the two great English-speaking peoples. . . . The stupendous revolution now going on in China is an additional reason why we should work together." [86] While he was president he once told Lee that it would be well for London and Washington to keep in touch day by day on the Chinese situation "so that our two countries could act exactly on the same lines." [87] Roosevelt and his friends continued to watch the phenomenon of China closely and with their own welfare in mind, and they were not reassured. In June, 1913, Bryce wrote from Mukden: "Every one agrees that China is as unfit for republican institutions as any country can be, but the chances of the restoration of the monarchy are slim. . . . The Legislature consists of men nearly all of whom are inexperienced and most of them young." It was Bryce's judgment that the Chinese were best left to sort out their own problems with "the less foreign intervention the better." [88] Assessing conditions on the mainland, he wrote from Tokyo the next month: "The position in China is most obscure. Anything may happen." [89] Roosevelt agreed as to fact and hope. "I have never believed that there was the slightest chance of a republic as the English-speaking people understand the term succeeding in China," he told Bryce. "But I had hoped there would be some kind of change that would permit the necessary evolution to proceed in China as an evolution and not a revolution." [90] The possibility that China might be devoured by one of the Powers compounded such fears, the prospect of which Brooks Adams had warned some years before.

Many of the disquieting thoughts Roosevelt and others entertained in the late 1890's, especially with respect to China, were stimulated by Brooks Adams. In *The Law of Civilization and Decay* he advanced the thesis, lugubrious indeed to the Anglo-Americans, that the center of power-political gravity would soon shift from the Atlantic nations to the Orient. According to this interpretation in the East modern techniques of industry would mate with the millions of Asia to create the national colossus of the future. This prospect was so thoroughly inimical to the English-speaking peoples that Roosevelt and Spring Rice both rejected it outright. Spring Rice castigated the Adams book. "I

don't approve of that way of writing history," he told TR.

I'm sick of theories. Everyone has a new prescription for humanity and a new diagnosis. They all begin with the Roman Empire and point out resemblances. The Roman Empire fell because there was no one left to fight for it; as long as we are born and live and are prepared to fight in sufficient numbers, I don't see that the present world is much like the age of the Antonines. At any rate the Roosevelt family are numerous and warlike.[91]

In the overall, however, Spring Rice remained as downhearted regarding China as he was in the case of Russia. Indeed, he saw the two problems to be in reality a single difficulty. He indulged his thoughts.

How interested you must be in China. The defence, as Brooks Adams would say, has now become sharper than the attack—owing to the new guns, and we shan't be able to treat small or weak nations as we used to. The result is interesting in several ways. The Russians for instance are immensely encouraged and say perhaps they may be able to easily maintain their independence. . . . On the other hand any civilized nation that can arm large bodies of semi-civilized people has a great advantage and it's plain in the possession of territory in China, and that is Russia. If any other power were to try they would have difficulty in maintaining an isolated colony against the *mass* of China. . . . This would be a bad thing for the world or China as the Russians have a wonderful knack of securing law and order. . . . The menace to the world becomes very great as the whole *mass* of Asia can be directed towards Europe. America has nothing to fear except a probable destruction of trade. . . . For Russia, the Russian soldier, diplomat, merchant—are ready to make any sacrifice. (As for the English in China, the Russian retort is: "You are merchants, we are conquerors.")[92]

Notwithstanding his dislike of Brooks Adams's predictions, events as Spring Rice judged them seemed to point in the same direction as Adams had foretold.

While Roosevelt and Spring Rice both dismissed the Adams thesis—"absolutely false" argued TR—their concentration on the hard facts of contemporary events did not prevent them from pondering the future of their race. When in Berlin in the 1890's Spring Rice busied himself "asking questions and collecting figures. It seems that all the experts agree that the main cause of the destruction of the Roman Empire was a failure of population, and this may have arisen from a variety of causes as to which there is some discrepancy. But of the fact there is no question." Whereupon in characteristic fashion he proceeded to expound to Roosevelt the possible parallels between ancient Rome and the modern states.[93] TR refused to draw the more obvious inferences and once again warned his friend of the too easy analogy. "Our civilization is far more widely extended than the early civilizations, and in consequence, there is much less chance for evil tendencies to

[86] Roosevelt to Lee, July 25, 1900, *Roosevelt Letters* 2: p. 1362.
[87] Roosevelt to Lee, Nov. 5, 1906, Lee Papers.
[88] Bryce to Roosevelt, June 28, 1913, Bryce Papers.
[89] Bryce to Roosevelt, July 13, 1913, *ibid.*
[90] Roosevelt to Bryce, Aug. 28, 1913, *ibid.*

[91] Spring Rice to Roosevelt, July 1, 1896, Spring Rice Papers.
[92] Spring Rice to Roosevelt, Aug. 9, 1900, Roosevelt Papers. (Italics in original.)
[93] Spring Rice to Roosevelt, May 1, 1897, Spring Rice Papers.

work universally through all its parts." He was more concerned about the consequences of an overconcentration of political power and a maldistribution of national wealth, both in America and England. As for virility "there are still great waste spaces which the English-speaking peoples undoubtedly have the vigor to fill." [94] But Spring Rice was obdurate. "In China as in Constantinople we can never hope to exercise a salutary influence on Government," he wrote from his Persian station. "The reasons are manifold of course. But I am convinced one reason is that the great neighboring Empire will not and can not allow a wise or civilized development. It must have rotten soil to grow in." [95] The deeper source of his concern was not alone the power of the Russians but the condition of the Anglo-American race, or at least its British branch.

The function of race was one prominent feature of the *weltpolitik* of Roosevelt and his friends. Belief in the premier quality of their race was one of their common commitments. When doubts about its vitality arose, the most serious implications were involved. In turn this vitality was related to the use of force, a willingness to utilize force in order to maintain political institutions at home and international leadership and prestige as well. Spring Rice especially was depressed by what he thought was a weakening of the Anglo-American race for this amounted to an unwillingness or an inability to fight either for one's national interest or for what was right. From St. Petersburg in December, 1904, he wrote Edith Carow Roosevelt that he had reluctantly concluded that his government had "a very big voice and a very small stick. I wonder if we are getting soft and cowardly? I think sometimes we must be, when I read about the Japs and the Russians and how they fight." [96] Roosevelt, seemingly always ready to agree in principle, continued to resist Spring Rice's gloomy estimate based on contemporary facts. Years before when the two men had discussed the race question in detail he had stated a basic position that did not significantly alter with the passing years. "As long as the birth rate exceeds the death rate and as long as the people of a nation will fight, and show some capacity for self-restraint and self-guidance in political affairs," he insisted to Spring Rice, he was not unduly worried. [97] Roosevelt was not indifferent to the possible faltering of their race; his own understanding of history allowed for the rise and fall of mighty nations. He simply did not take it to be a pertinent consideration for the English-speaking peoples, and especially for the Americans, at the onset of the twentieth century. As for "the men we adopt as well as to the children we beget, it must

be remembered that actually we keep increasing at about twice the rate as the Russians. . . . I can not see that we have lost vigor compared to what we were a century ago. If anything, I think we have gained." TR based his observations on those numerous individuals he had met as menbers of the New York police force, the ratings of the United States Navy, and the workers he had talked with on countless construction projects. "These men are not effete," he told Spring Rice, "and if you compare them with the Russians (and of course exactly the same thing would be true if you compared the Russians with corresponding Englishmen) . . . these men would out-build, out-administer, and out-fight any Russian you could find." "Of course the English and the Americans are less ruthless and have the disadvantage of civilization," he allowed, adding, "I think that though the people of the English-speaking races may have to divide the future with the Slav, yet they will get rather more than their fair share." [98] Not surprisingly Spring Rice was unpersuaded. His contrary judgments, he told his correspondent, were grounded on a book no less fundamental than *Burke's Peerage*—"a most interesting genealogical collection," which told how the race declined as luxury increased.[99] "We are as a nation (that is, on this side of the Atlantic) rather tired and inclined to take a satisfied view of the present. You are familiar with the weary elegance of certain Bostonians. I don't know whether the race is getting exhausted or what it is." [100] Roosevelt, admitting cause for concern, preferred to be cheerful about the future. ". . . The Settlement of North America and Australia goes on and the remaining waste spaces of the two continents will be practically occupied in our own life time." As TR confessed, he himself had been so active and so busy that he had little time or taste for pessimism.[101]

The disposition to think of the large problems of the Anglo-American race on the part of the Roosevelt circle had an analogue in their apprehensiveness about the elites of England and America. "I don't know how far English society should be judged by its top layers," Spring Rice remarked to Roosevelt. "What is rotten: heartless, crazy for money and excitment, led by politicians, and incapable of sustained and patient effort, very much ruled by young women who make noises and talk philosophy and politics like the ladies before the French Revolution. . . . I wonder about your rich?" [102] Once again TR felt constrained to offer some agreement, but typically refused to be discouraged by his

[94] Roosevelt to Spring Rice, May 29, 1897, *Roosevelt Letters* 1: p. 628.

[95] Spring Rice to Roosevelt, Jan. 31, 1901, Roosevelt Papers.

[96] Spring Rice to Edith Carow Roosevelt, Dec. 6, 1904, Gwynn, 1929: 1: p. 437.

[97] Roosevelt to Spring Rice, Aug. 5, 1896, *Roosevelt Letters* 1: p. 554.

[98] Roosevelt to Spring Rice, Aug. 13, 1897, *ibid.* 1: pp. 648–649.

[99] Spring Rice to Roosevelt, May, 1897, Gwynn, 1929: 1: p. 215.

[100] Spring Rice to Roosevelt, Jan. 31, 1901, Roosevelt Papers.

[101] Roosevelt to Spring Rice, March 16, 1901, *Roosevelt Letters* 2: p. 15.

[102] Spring Rice to Roosevelt, June 15, 1901, Roosevelt Papers.

friend's strictures.[103] Not many years later, however, Roosevelt wrote to George O. Trevelyan of the evil tendencies in their societies which the English-speaking people had to combat; his mood had become an uneasy one.

In England, in the United States, in Canada and Australia, and in the English parts of South Africa, there is more and more a tendency for the men who speak English to gather into the cities and towns. Now in the past the man on the farm has always proved to be the man who, in the last analysis, did the best service in governing himself in times of peace, and also in fighting in times of war. The city-bred folk, and especially where the cities are of enormous size, have not yet shown that they can adequately fill the place left vacant by the dwindling country population. Moreover the declining birth-rate among the people is an ugly thing.

And yet, despite all these forebodings, Roosevelt could not refrain from stating his belief that the English-speaking races enjoyed more human happiness than any other people.[104] His New World optimism was deeply rooted.

Roosevelt's English correspondence sounded other notes, more positive and no less suggestive of the function of race. Arthur Lee once explained to TR that one of his motives for entering public life had been, in effect, a racial one. "In my humble opinion," he wrote, "the future relations between England and America are going to form the joint upon which the whole future of the Anglo-Saxon race will hinge, and I ask nothing better than to essay the part of a drop of oil to lubricate that joint." [105] Indicative of the growing intimacy of the two nations he found that Roosevelt was the "first President since Lincoln in whom the English 'man in the street' has taken a real interest." [106] When TR visited British settlements in Africa in 1909 he recounted to Lee: "Your settlers here reminded me so much of my beloved Westerners that I felt absolutely at home among them; and unless I am mistaken they cordially received me as a natural friend." [107] As he observed to James Bryce regarding his reception in British East Africa: "It was rather difficult to remember I was not at home." [108]

When Roosevelt wrote about American politics in his friendly letters, he more than once took the time to comment on how the Anglo-Saxon element in the American peoples came quickly to dominate other strains. "A curious thing is that I think those Americans who were Anglo-Saxon by adoption, as it were, are quite as strong about the unity of the two peoples as any others," he told Spring Rice in 1899. "The

third generation Germans feel far more akin to England as a rule than they do to Germany." [109] Roosevelt was grateful that the 1900 presidential campaign made no appeal to "class, race, caste or national prejudice or international antipathies," taking this as proof that racial and cultural assimilation was reasonably effective.[110] Yet he was realistic for he did not imagine that all Germans had totally forsaken their fatherland upon coming to America or that the Irish-Americans could forget or forgive centuries of English oppression.[111] Somewhat humorously TR made his point when in 1914 a statue of Queen Victoria was proposed for Central Park in New York City, part of the abortive celebration of "one hundred years of peace" between the United States and Great Britain. He looked upon such a gesture as the kind of sentimentality that ought not to characterize dealings between the two countries, saying in a letter to Arthur Lee that a marble figure of Victoria would furnish "a steady occupation for the police force in protecting it from Celtic enthusiasts whose life ambition would be to blow it up." [112] In fact, Roosevelt was an unsparing opponent of sentimentality in whatever guise in so far as Anglo-American friendship was concerned. "I have never gushed over England," was a statement he was fond of making. The whole idea of commemorating "one hundred years of peace" between the two peoples he dismisses as "simply preposterous." [113] Nevertheless, though the process of ethnic amalgamation was slow and not miracle working, and though there were serious obstacles in the achievement of *homo Americanus*, assimilation did come about. Roosevelt had the American experience exactly in mind when he thought what British victory in the Boer War would mean.

Under English rulers, as has been shown in Cape Colony, the Dutch will have exactly the same rights as the English. . . . Then will come peace and the Afrikander will grow up like the Australian, the Canadian and the American. Here [in the United States] our people of different race origin fused very soon.[114]

Strachey and Roosevelt in particular were conscious of the power of the English language to dominate other tongues and the tendency of the English common law and standards of legal right and wrong to prevail over non-English ways.[115]

The Japanese-Americans were the one serious exception to Roosevelt's concept of ethnic assimilation,

[103] Roosevelt to Spring Rice, July 3, 1901, *Roosevelt Letters* 2: p. 108.
[104] Roosevelt to Trevelyan, March 9, 1905, *ibid.* 4: pp. 1134–1135.
[105] Lee to Roosevelt, July 19, 1900, Roosevelt Papers.
[106] Lee to Roosevelt, Dec. 17, 1901, *ibid.*
[107] Roosevelt to Lee, Oct. 6, 1909, *Roosevelt Letters* 2: p. 32.
[108] Roosevelt to Bryce, April 2, 1910, Bryce Papers.

[109] Roosevelt to Spring Rice, Feb. 14, 1899, *Roosevelt Letters* 1: p. 944.
[110] Roosevelt to Strachey, Nov. 19, 1900, *ibid.* 2: p. 1424.
[111] For example, Roosevelt to Spring Rice, Aug. 11, 1899, *ibid.* 2: pp. 1049–1050.
[112] Roosevelt to Lee, July 7, 1913, *ibid.* 7: p. 739.
[113] *Ibid.*
[114] Roosevelt to Spring Rice, Jan. 27, 1900, *ibid.* 2: p. 1146; Roosevelt to Lee, Jan. 30, 1900, *ibid.* 2: p. 1152.
[115] Strachey to Roosevelt, March 19, 1915, Strachey Papers; Roosevelt to Spring Rice, July 20, 1900, *Roosevelt Letters* 2: p. 1359.

the beating of all the various races into the one great American race. Within the British Empire Australia and Canada faced somewhat the same problems as the United States. Large numbers of Japanese immigrants entered those areas, so that London and Washington inclined to look upon the situation with similar misgivings.[116] Referring specifically to the flow of Japanese into areas controlled by English speaking peoples, TR observed to Strachey: "It is curious how in our two governments parallel problems always arise."[117] Roosevelt had undoubted admiration for the Japanese. Mass migration of Japanese laborers into the United States (and by inference into Australia and Canada) was another matter altogether. To both Lee and Strachey he asserted "there should be no immigration in mass of Orientals where the English-speaking peoples now form or will form the populations of the future."[118] He was clearly afraid that Orientals, in view of their distinctiveness in culture and outlook defy assimilation, and so their entry into the English nations must be rigorously limited.[119] As for the Japanese already in the United States, "we shall treat [them] in an exact equality with the people of Europe."[120] Looking backward from 1913 on the problems created by large-scale Japanese immigrations into English-speaking lands, James Bryce wrote TR:

personally I believe it would have been better if our people and yours had frankly taken the attitude which I took six or seven years ago, and announced it as part of a reciprocal policy between Japan and the United States and the free commonwealths of the British Empire that there should be no mass immigration to one country from another. Just as long as there is such immigration or settlement in mass, there is bound to be trouble.[121]

Bryce further noted, while visiting in Japan in 1913, "a good deal of irritation still existing about the California Land Act," with a possible weakening of good relations between Japan and America as a consequence.[122]

Additional evidence of this attitude on the part of the Roosevelt set was contained in the correspondence between Arthur Lee and TR at the time of the Mackenzie King mission to London in 1908. The Canadians themselves were sufficiently aroused by the Japanese influx into British Columbia to dispatch a special emissary to England with a view toward obtaining British support for immigration restrictions. The United States was especially interested in Canadian regulations because large numbers of Japanese were entering the country from the Canadian Pacific area. Wanting to take a step beyond the "Gentlemen's Agreement" (1907), the president sought to use the services of MacKenzie King in a quasi-official manner to convey to London the American position and intention. Since Japan and England were allies, TR maneuvered to have Downing Street bring pressure on Japan to prevent continued migration of Japanese laborers. In the end Roosevelt failed but the Roosevelt-Lee letters confirmed beyond dispute the racial suspicions they harbored. In describing one of his meetings with MacKenzie King before the latter left for England, the president informed Lee that he had advised concerted action by London and Washington which, while reaffirming friendship with Japan, looked upon further migrations on a large scale into the Pacific coastal areas as "highly inadvisable. [There] must be a complete cessation of the emigration of Japanese laborers to the English speaking countries surrounding the Pacific." Otherwise, Roosevelt told Lee, the sternest measures would have to be taken. Recognizing that this might strain Anglo-Japanese relations grievously he asked the Canadian emissary to urge joint action by the two governments "in the interests of lasting peace and good will between Japan and the English-speaking peoples."[123] Lee replied to the president that he would do "everything in his power" to facilitate Mackenzie King's mission. He related a long talk he had had with Balfour, "who is keenly interested in the subject of intercourse between the white and yellow races and holds very decided and advanced views as to the absolute necessity of keeping them apart. He entirely endorses your opinions on this point and heartily supports [your] policy. . . ."[124] After the completion of King's visit Lee reported that the Canadian "found no difference of opinion as to your main principles that a complete halt should be called on the immigration of laborers into English speaking countries from Japan, or any other Oriental country, and vice-versa, and that if necessary the English speaking communities should cooperate to make the exclusions effective." There were, he observed, "no real joints in our armour," hardly an accurate summation in light of Great Britain's decision to ignore the problem for the sake of Anglo-Japanese cooperation.[125]

The utilization of force, and when imperative, a resort to all-out war, formed integral parts of the *weltpolitik* Roosevelt and his English correspondents elaborated and espoused. American deployment of large numbers of army regulars to subdue the Philippines and the massing of imperial troops against the Boers leave no doubt of the willingness of the Anglo-Americans to use armed might and the letters of TR and his friends attest to the "logic" of its place in the world order. Echoing a Rooseveltian phrase, Spring Rice

[116] Strachey to Roosevelt, Dec. 31, 1906, Strachey Papers.
[117] Roosevelt to Strachey, Feb. 22, 1907, *Roosevelt Letters* 5: p. 597.
[118] Roosevelt to Lee, March 7, 1908, *ibid.* 6: p. 965.
[119] Roosevelt to George O. Trevelyan, Sept. 12, 1905, *ibid,* 5: p. 22.
[120] Roosevelt to Strachey, Feb. 22, 1907, *ibid.* 5: pp. 597–598.
[121] Bryce to Roosevelt, Aug. 28, 1913, Bryce Papers.
[122] Bryce to Roosevelt, July 14, 1913, *ibid.*

[123] Roosevelt to Lee, Feb. 2, 1908, *Roosevelt Letters* 4: pp. 919–921, *passim.*
[124] Lee to Roosevelt, Feb. 21, 1908, Roosevelt Papers.
[125] Lee to Roosevelt, March 31, 1908, *ibid.*

once exclaimed: "don't make a diplomatic request *unless* and until you are ready with the big stick after the soft words." [126] Spokesmen for peace among nations through the creation of some sort of international mechanism had become more popular and more respected in the first years of the twentieth century. In consequence those who continued to insist upon a role for military power in their public philosophy often found themselves arguing their cause in response to the "peace advocates." St. Loe Strachey, flaying the "peace at any price" mentality, stated his case for the use of force in a letter to Roosevelt in 1906, wherein elements of *realpolitik* mingled easily with higher motives.

It is astonishing that with all history staring them in their faces, people seem to imagine that civil liberty is something that comes with nature and needs no protecting. Yet in truth our liberties and the rights of man to enjoy political freedom can only be maintained by a conscious effort, and by the fact that in the last resort men are willing to die to maintain their rights. [127]

Strachey analyzed this problem in terms of the difficulties which any American leader might have in arousing the nation to a state of military readiness. He thought the United States might well be "drowned in security." "I am afraid," he wrote Roosevelt, "that the people of the United States are to a certain extent in this position. Their immense power, wealth and happiness have inclined them to think that nothing could ever go wrong, and they need take no precautions." [128] Roosevelt was a deadly foe of the "peace at any price" men and a resolute champion of "the manlier virtues and whatever tends toward effective nation defense." [129] Still, what Strachey, Roosevelt, and the others had in mind was war to protect their internal political arrangements and not simply armed power to keep their favorable world position. As Roosevelt made plain to George O. Trevelyan in a discussion of arms limitation: "I have no sympathy with those who fear to fight for a just cause, and who are not willing to prepare so that they can at need fight effectively. But neither have I any sympathy with those who would lightly undergo the chance of war in a spirit of mere frivolity, or of mere truculence." [130] TR's view of war was in fact more balanced than might be supposed. "As you know I am not a peace at any price man," he confided to Strachey at the time of the Russo-Japanese War, "but I have grown to feel an increasing horror for pointless and of course still more, for unjust war. A continuation of the struggle [of the Russians and the Japanese] was utterly pointless and a hideous slaughter of gallant men." [131]

War was a serious business because of the consequences of fighting or choosing not to fight. Strachey spoke his anxiety of what would happen were the world to go "peace at any price mad." "The result would be that we should ultimately be dominated by aristocracies and that men of the type of Napoleon would spring on the backs of the people and ride them at will." A note of moral superiority sounded as Strachey went on.

I should like to see armaments reduced, but I am I confess a little anxious as to whether our Government may not do something foolish at the Hague Conference. If we pledge ourselves to disarmament no doubt we shall loyally carry out our plans but I feel by no means sure that the great continental Powers can be trusted to do this. [132]

Nor does one have to search far to identify the source of this superior attitude. English and American "liberty and good government" had "to be defended against the forces of autocracy and obscurantism still very strong in the world. To my mind nothing is so silly as the notion that because a man has learnt the use of arms that we must assume he will make a bad use of this knowledge." [133] Such were Strachey's thoughts given Roosevelt at the same time as he praised the withdrawal of the British Fleet from North Atlantic and Caribbean waters as a sign that the two Anglo-American navies would patrol the world together. Arthur Lee said much the same thing, even more directly, in reference to joint Anglo-American naval strategy.

I suppose nothing is *impossible* in this world—even the suicide of the English speaking races—but I am an optimist by profession and I rejoice in the thought that within the next few years there will be 75 first class battleships afloat, all manned by English speaking sailors and constituting the most formidable argument or guarantee for universal peace that the world has even seen. [134]

The sense of moral superiority was again apparent. Strachey and Lee and Roosevelt all assumed that the Anglo-Americans had acquired that habit of self-mastery which enabled them, as distinct from other races, to use force with wisdom and justice.

If necessary, however, a combined Anglo-American fleet would be ready for war. Trevelyan, Lee, and Roosevelt were all naval enthusiasts and had served at one time or another as civilians responsible for the naval preparedness of their countries. Trevelyan for one was concerned with naval efficiency in light of financial efficiency, once the Anglo-German naval race had been fairly joined. To Roosevelt in 1906 he took a stand against the construction of "vast and vastly expensive ships." "If *your* naval battles and the Japanese and Russian naval battles prove anything, it is that the number of *hits* made by quick firing, numerous guns of a certain size and caliber is what wins a battle." What was required, he added, was "a real force." [135] With

---

[126] Spring Rice to Roosevelt, Nov. 9, 1904, Gwynn, 1929: 2: p. 436. (Italics in original.)

[127] Strachey to Roosevelt, Sept. 23, 1906, Strachey Papers.

[128] Strachey to Roosevelt, Aug. 29, 1906, *ibid.*

[129] Roosevelt to Strachey, Sept. 7, 1906, *ibid.*

[130] Roosevelt to Trevelyan, Sept. 9, 1906, *Roosevelt Letters* 5: p. 400.

[131] Roosevelt to Strachey, Sept. 11, 1905, Strachey Papers.

[132] Strachey to Roosevelt, Sept. 21, 1906, *ibid.*

[133] Strachey to Roosevelt, Aug. 29, 1906, Roosevelt Papers.

[134] Lee to Roosevelt, May 24, 1905, *ibid.*

[135] Trevelyan to Roosevelt, Sept. 27, 1906, *ibid.*

the passing years and the intensification of the naval arms race, Roosevelt confessed himself to Arthur Lee "almost as anxious as you to have the British fleet kept to the highest point of efficiency. It is a great guarantee for the peace of the world."[136] Believing as he did, Lee valued the president's encouragement and related to him his conviction that the German navy was a menace "with its openly avowed object of contesting the command-of-the-sea with us." He went on to lament that British public opinion was not sufficiently aware of the threat the German navy posed, and that it was hard work making them aware. But at last he thought the German threat was beginning to be comprehended by the public at large, he wrote TR in 1908.[137] Roosevelt, cognizant of the problems of leadership in free societies, complimented Lee. "I am glad indeed to hear from you that the British people are alive to the necessities of national defense," asserting once more that it was a "good thing . . . keeping England and America closer together, which as you know is something I always have peculiarly at heart."[138]

Roosevelt and his friends were fully wedded to the belief that the English and American nations should and could get along amicably because of their common commitments. Roosevelt once spoke of the prospects of war with England as a "nightmare," "out of the question," "practically impossible."[139] Somewhat self-consciously Arthur Lee had entered British politics in 1900 to dispel the ignorance between the two peoples which he pronounced "unbelievably dense."[140] In one letter written in 1903 he referred to his nickname in the House of Commons, "the member for America," saying "I hope it will do no harm to have one member of the Government at least who knows and cares something about your country."[141] On Roosevelt's retirement from the presidency, Bryce sent him a warm letter of congratulations which included the following passage:

One thing I can't tell you and that is how great and constant a pleasure it has been to me to represent my country to yours when you were the latter's head and to know that never was the relationship so intimate and so trustful between the two peoples that ought to be the closest of friends and fellow-workers.[142]

When Lee learned that Roosevelt had been invited to give the Romanes Lecture at Oxford he wrote at once: "I devoutly hope that the idea of the solidarity and cooperation of the English speaking races may be dragged in somehow in your address."[143] For his part, Roosevelt spoke to Strachey along the same line, after the editor of the *Spectator* had used the columns of that journal to defend TR as a friend of England during the controversy over the Arbitration Treaty of 1911. "I think I can honestly say that I have done everything I possibly could, while I was President, while I was Governor and since, to strengthen the bands of good will, regard and sympathy between the two countries and to show how fundamentally alike we are," he told Strachey.[144] Such a comment undoubtedly meant a great deal to Strachey as he was the most sentimental of all the correspondents in matters pertaining to Anglo-American friendship.[145] No one made more frequent reference to the blood ties between the two peoples, nor was more likely to violate Roosevelt's Eleventh Commandment regarding England: Thou shalt not slop over.[146] Yet in the end it was not sentiment that cemented the entente but morality, the moral excellence which Roosevelt and his friends took to be the unique possession of their race. None of the correspondents was likely to write more movingly of the moral unity of the race than Cecil Spring Rice. At a time when much of world opinion was openly hostile to England because of pressure on the Boers in South Africa, Spring Rice poured out his thoughts to his friend.

I am afraid it will sound like ordinary English hypocrisy and especially from a person of my profession who did not at once disapprove of the Jameson raid; but then I was in Germany at the time. What I was going to say was the trite remark that true patriotism ought to be one's love for one's relations. If they do wrong, it is a personal shame and disgrace to oneself. But that can never justify except in extreme cases, an abandonment. But I should think that an honorable man should be as much grieved if his brother turned thief as if he had turned bankrupt. One ought to treasure one's country's reputation as one would one's wife. Probably both our countries have got a reputation for being humbugs by very sincerely professing this doctrine. It has paid. And because it has paid, our enemies say that we cared for the profit and not for the principle. I think if we hadn't believed in the principles we should never have won the profit. I daresay the British part of the common inheritance is going down hill; all the more reason to look after the other. I don't believe it will prosper unless it keeps up a human heart and noble aims. You are one of the people who can water that particular plant, and God speed you![147]

In many ways Spring Rice was correct. The English and the Americans were part of the same family. Through much of Anglo-American history down to 1898 it was a fact often reluctantly admitted on both sides of the Atlantic, and it remained so for many

[136] Roosevelt to Lee, Aug. 7, 1908, *Roosevelt Letters* 6: p. 1159.
[137] Lee to Roosevelt, Sept. 6, 1908, Lee Papers.
[138] Roosevelt to Lee, Dec. 20, 1908, *Roosevelt Letters* 6: p. 1432.
[139] Roosevelt to Lee, June 6, 1905, *ibid.* 6: p. 1207.
[140] Lee to Roosevelt, July 19, 1900, Roosevelt Papers.
[141] Lee to Roosevelt, Nov. 22, 1903, *ibid.*
[142] Bryce to Roosevelt, March 6, 1909, Bishop, 1920: 2: p. 135.
[143] Lee to Roosevelt, Oct. 4, 1908, Roosevelt Papers.

[144] Roosevelt to Strachey, March 26, 1912, *Roosevelt Letters* 7: p. 531.
[145] For example, Strachey to Roosevelt, Oct. 1, 1904, Roosevelt Papers; Strachey to Roosevelt, April 3, 1906, Strachey Papers.
[146] Roosevelt to Lee, July 7, 1913, *Roosevelt Letters* 7: p. 739.
[147] Spring Rice to Roosevelt, Nov. 3, 1897, Gwynn, 1929: 2: p. 235.

people, even after the great rapprochement was underway. But for the elites of both nations, of which Theodore Roosevelt and his friends were representative, the usefulness and attractiveness of the friendship became increasingly apparent with the first years of the twentieth century. The common commitment took on new significance as successive events demonstrated the value of cooperation and accord betwen the two nations. Save for the accummulation of events after 1898, the English and American peoples may have remained more or less apart in matters of international cooperation, and certainly in so far as a wartime alliance was concerned. But given developments—an enlarged United States interest in the Caribbean and involvement in the Far East in combination with Britain's abandonment of splendid isolation as the world balance of power shifted —the rapprochement grew naturally according to a common heritage as well as opportely, out of mutual advantage. Events themselves between 1898 and 1914 would give a more decisive shape and a more exact definition to the form of the alliance, subsumed as it was by a spirit of Anglo-American unity.

III. DIPLOMACY

It is an easy matter to date the beginning of the Anglo-American diplomatic rapprochement. The year 1898 was *annus mirabilis,* signaling a shift away from historic antagonisms and toward historic cooperation. The bellicose stance the United States took toward England in the Venezuelan boundary dispute of 1895 was replaced by a cordiality born of British sympathy for America in her war with Spain. Theodore Roosevelt thought the shift a dramatic one. "The attitude of England in 1898 worked a complete revolution in my feelings and the attitude of the continent at that time opened my eyes to the other side," he told Arthur Lee.[1] The succession of events that ensued down to the eve of the First World War brought the United States and Great Britain closer together. Reflecting on the meaning of these international developments, and at times helping to guide them, Roosevelt and his English friends came slowly to see the more exact nature of their special relationship, both its strengths and its limitations. A relationship of two fully sovereign nations not bound together by any formal treaty, its resilience was due to the informality of the understanding with each nation, at given points, pursuing her own priority of goals. In so acting the United States and Great Britain were influenced, nevertheless, by an implicit conception of the general identity of Anglo-American interests. As early as 1905 Roosevelt had written to Strachey: "I regard all danger of any trouble between the United States and Great Britain as over, I think for ever. This is only another way of saying that every free people should strive to combine ability to defend its own rights with a hearty regard for the rights of others."[2] The consideration that seemed destined to obviate future strife was the "free people" character of the English and the Americans, a concept evoking race, history, and common institutions. Free peoples might not always agree on the disposition of an issue between them. America and England were deeply divided by the Alaska boundary controversy, for example, though more typically their divisions were not so pronounced. For an appreciation of the Anglo-American resolution of difficulties, large and small, the thoughts of Roosevelt and his English friends were no less important than the means of settlement, for behind the diplomacy stood a willingness to compromise, a willingness composed of mutual regard and mutual need. Roosevelt's English correspondence gives convincing evidence of this. In the face of events the two nations learned the acceptable limits of friendship, and of sovereignty. An actual working out of a solution to a particular problem evinced the viability of the relationship, so that by the outbreak of general war in 1914 the rapprochement had sufficiently matured to withstand the frontal test of any understanding between nations, a conflict of ultimate self-interest.

The rapprochement commenced on a note of war and friendship. American insistence on war with Spain to rid Cuba of Spanish mismanagement, along with whatever possibilities for an extension of power the conflict might provide, combined with British acquiescence if not outright approval of American action against Spain. In October, 1897, Lord Salisbury assured Secretary of State John Hay that British commitments in Cuba were purely commercial and that Her Majesty's Government would favor any American policy aimed at pacifying Cuba. At the time English public opinion was decidedly pro-American. In the diplomatic maneuvering that followed in the wake of the *Maine* disaster Downing Street remained essentially noncommittal, despite the efforts of Sir Julian Pauncefote, the British ambassador in Washington, to show the Americans that world opinion was against a Spanish-American war. Europe was openly hostile to the United States, but Britain came to view the war as the Americans did. Once hostilities got underway public opinion in England remained pro-American, while the government, ostensibly neutral, managed its policies in a number of ways for the benefit of the United States.[3]

Theodore Roosevelt, and in his judgment Americans at large, were impressed favorably by Britain's apparently friendly attitude during the crisis, and they

---

[1] Roosevelt to Lee, July 25, 1900, *Roosevelt Letters* 5: p. 1362.

[2] Roosevelt to Strachey, Sept. 2, 1905, Strachey Papers; see also Roosevelt to Strachey, June 6, 1905, *Roosevelt Letters* 4: p. 1207.

[3] For an informative account of the British attitude toward the war see C. S. Campbell, 1957; pp. 25–55; J.A.S. Grenville, 1964: pp. 199–217 is also enlightening. For a useful summary of favorable British reaction to United States expansion based on a wide survey of opinion consult Geoffrey Seed, "British Reactions to American Imperialism Reflected in Journals of Opinion, 1898–1900," *Pol. Sci. Quart.* 73: pp. 254–272.

gave little credence to the story, some years later, that it was Germany and not England that had prevented a strong diplomatic note from the Powers protesting United States military intentions respecting Cuba. Roosevelt graphically explained the American reaction to Arthur Lee.

I feel very strongly that the Engish-speaking peoples are now closer together than for a century and a quarter, and that every effort should be made to keep them together; for their interests are really fundamentally the same, and they are far more closely akin, not merely in blood, but in feeling and in principles, than either is akin to any other people in the world. I think we are both of us stronger for what has happened in the last eight months.[4]

TR and his friends consciously viewed the Spanish war as the start of Anglo-American diplomatic cooperation because the war and its ramifications persuaded them that in the future their respective national interests were more likely to complement than to conflict. In the western hemisphere American power would thwart German ambitions while leaving England undisturbed in her possessions. In the Far East the presence of the United States would work to stabilize what threatened to be a highly unstable situation. Roosevelt, for example, utilized the British attitude of friendship in 1898 during his campaign for the vice-presidency in 1900. He told Spring Rice that he made "hearty acknowledgement" of it and "contrasted [it] with the attitude of the continental European powers." But, he insisted, this did not make him an Anglo-maniac. Britain's friendship had simply worked to promote American advantage, which was his premier concern, more readily.[5] As hard-nosed as Roosevelt wanted his position judged, and as realistic as it in fact was, he associated the Spanish war with an awareness of the kinship of England and America. In a letter, again to Spring Rice, dated August 11, 1899, he wrote that he was inclined to "the view of my beloved Lt. Parker of the Gatlings whom I overheard telling the Russian Naval Attaché at Santiago that 'the two branches of the Anglo-Saxon race had come together, and that together we can whip the world, Prince, we can whip the world!'"[6] Spring Rice, mindful of England's posture in 1898, recalled to TR some two years after the war that all "Europe was philo-Spanish. . . . The sudden and wholly unexpected sympathy of England for America dashed Germany's hopes of using its free hand. It was clear," he continued, "England would not acquiesce in a concert of Europe to deprive America of the fruits of her conquests." According to Spring Rice, Germany had subsequently sought to punish England for her friendship with America in 1898.[7] Well after the end of the war Arthur Lee informed

Roosevelt that one of the ill effects for the Conservative party had been that British assistance to the United States before and during the war was represented by the Liberal opposition as actuated by "base motives," that the Conservatives would "grovel to any extent to keep in with America." This was "utter nonsense" he added. "All our best people wish to grow closer to America." If Roosevelt could but make a brief visit to England, he would see for himself, argued Lee, "how earnestly and really disinterestedly" England favored America.[8]

The moral superiority which Roosevelt and his friends often exhibited was undisguised in a letter from TR to James Bryce a few weeks before the outbreak of hostilities between the United States and Spain. Roosevelt wanted to justify impending American action to an Englishman who entertained doubts about the enterprize. "I feel that we have been derelict in not interfering in behalf of Cuba for precisely the same reason that I feel you were derelict in not interfering in behalf of Armenia—and I never preach to others what I don't, when I have the power, advocate doing myself. We should drive Spain from the Western World," he told Bryce, because "for the last three years in Cuba she has revived the policy and most of the methods of Alva and Torquemada."[9] Once the war was over, Roosevelt had no regrets as to its outcome. "I believed with all my heart in the war with Spain," he boasted to Bryce in November, 1898.[10] Bryce, however, was better able to think through the implications behind almost certain American success. With the battles fought and won his concern surfaced rapidly. Granting the stupendous American victories, Bryce was uneasy at the change of the United States to a colonial power.

The new enterprises you will enter on are enterprises for which your Constitution and government have not been formed, and mistakes may be made, many and serious, before you develop the institutions needed. Perhaps it is because we have had such a lot of experience, some of it most unsatisfactory with our tropical colonies, that I am more anxious to see the American people purify city government and do certain other jobs at home than to see them civilize the Malays and aborigines of Luzon.

Some of Bryce's other comments Roosevelt looked on more favorably.

What I hope you will do, [he continued] is to have a healthy despotism governing these tropical semi-savages and even Spanish creoles. No talk of suffrage or any such constitutional privileges for them, but steady government by the firmest, most honest men you can find, and no interference if possible by Congress when the firm and honest men have been found.

Having mixed caution with encouragement, Bryce concluded his letter on an appropriate Anglo-American

---

[4] Roosevelt to Lee, Nov. 25, 1898, *Roosevelt Letters* **2**: pp. 889–890.

[5] Roosevelt to Spring Rice, Nov. 19, 1900, *ibid.* **2**: p. 1423.

[6] Roosevelt to Spring Rice, Aug. 11, 1899, *ibid.* **2**: p. 1053.

[7] Spring Rice to Roosevelt, Sept. 3, 1900, Roosevelt Papers.

[8] Lee to Roosevelt, Nov. 2, 1900, *ibid.*

[9] Roosevelt to Bryce, March 31, 1896, *Roosevelt Letters* **2**: p. 807.

[10] Roosevelt to Bryce, Nov. 25, 1898, *ibid.* **2**: p. 889.

chord. "It is a happy result of the last six months that your people and ours seem nearer together in sympathy than ever before. You will have noticed that nearly every one here applauds your imperialistic new departure. We are here growing more imperialistic than ever." [11] Conservative or Liberal in Britain, the needs of empire sometimes transcended party lines, and Roosevelt found it possible to be on good terms with men from either political camp.[12]

Nonetheless Bryce's words were prophetic. The United States had to develop gradually a policy and a program for the Philippines. Eventually successful, it was no simple task to find the "firm, honest men," nor to keep Congress from interference. Roosevelt and Spring Rice discussed the problem. Spring Rice told his friend that he was frankly relieved when the United States had determined her intention to retain the Philippine Islands and to govern them.[13] As to the outcome of the experiment, Roosevelt admitted to some uneasy moments and foresaw the use of "plenty of troops" to get the Islands in "good shape." The successful governance of the Philippines he believed was "of infinite importance to us as a nation and to our future career." [14] After a year of blundering, he wrote Spring Rice in December of 1899, "we at last seem to have things pretty well in hand, and I guess there will be no trouble of any serious kind save in administering the islands hereafter." [15] As American control over the Islands tightened, TR described to St. Loe Strachey "Philippine events . . . slowly working towards a proper solution, if only our people have patience enough to be willing to wait." [16] The British, too, were prepared to be patient, well pleased to have an effective partner in the Far East.

United States policy toward the *insurrectos* in the Philippines bore a striking similarity to British efforts to defeat the Boer rebels in South Africa. Roosevelt noted this in a letter to Spring Rice, pointing out that just as some American senators compared Aguinaldo, the Filipino rebel chief, to Washington so "it is possible taking a similar ground about the Boers," and added laconically, "and they can always quote Morely, Bryce, etc." [17] In the mind of Roosevelt, and many Englishmen as well, was a difference between Boer and Filipino which rendered the use of force against the former more difficult to justify. After the Jameson Raid, Spring

Rice wrote to Edith Carow Roosevelt: "I wonder if Theodore maintains his interest in S. African affairs and which way his sympathies go? We are all, officially, in transports of indignation at Jameson's proceedings: which are certainly without excuse. But he seems to be just the type of man Theodore writes about." [18] When hostilities were underway in earnest, however, Spring Rice unveiled a troubled English conscience. He confided to TR: "If I were not an Englishman I should certainly sympathize with the Boers—and we can't possibly complain if other people do it." [19] Spring Rice's attitude spoke the same uncertainty which Roosevelt and others of the circle of friends felt. Roosevelt spelled out his position in a letter to Spring Rice in December, 1899.

The Boers are belated Cromwellians, with many fine traits. . . . But it would be for the advantage of mankind to have English spoken south of the Zambesi, just as in New York, and as I told one of my fellow knickerbockers the other day, as we let the Uitlanders of old in here, I do not see why the same rule is not good enough for the Transvaal.[20]

Nonetheless the war made Roosevelt both sad and melancholy.[21] The grim fact was that "English spoken south of the Zambesi" had to be accomplished by force. Consequently, Roosevelt wrote Arthur Lee, "I wish you were able to place an overwhelming force in South Africa at once and get the thing over with as soon as possible." [22] Large segments of American opinion instinctively but inactively favored the Boer cause, while the American government kept a benevolent neutrality, all that England really wanted. Amid these circumstances, Roosevelt's sympathy for Britain was especially appreciated by those of his friends who favored suppression of the Boers.[23]

Granting the ability of Great Britain to defeat the Boers eventually, the larger concern of Roosevelt and others was the future of South Africa. Here the outlook was encouraging. "The last thing we want to do is to take any rights from the Boers," Strachey had written to his American friend early in 1900. The moment the military period is over we shall of course grant the most complete and democratic self-government. Not even the wildest jingo wants to turn the Boers into Outlanders." Strachey then went on to underscore certain comparisons between the American Civil War and the Boer War.

[11] Bryce to Roosevelt, Sept. 12, 1898, Bishop, 1920: 1: pp. 106–107.

[12] For a discussion of tensions as well as cooperation in Anglo-American relations, see D. C. Watt, "American and British Foreign Policy-Making Elites, from Joseph Chamberlain to Anthony Eden, 1895–1956," *Rev. of Pol.* 25: pp. 3–33.

[13] Spring Rice to Roosevelt, Nov. 15, 1898, Gwyn, 1929: 1: p. 269.

[14] Roosevelt to Spring Rice, Aug. 12, 1899, *Roosevelt Letters* 2: p. 1054.

[15] Roosevelt to Spring Rice, Dec. 2, 1899, *ibid.* 2: p. 1104.

[16] Roosevelt to Strachey, March 8, 1901, *ibid.* 3: p. 8.

[17] Roosevelt to Spring Rice, Jan. 27, 1900, *ibid.* 2: p. 1147.

[18] Spring Rice to Edith Carow Roosevelt, Feb. 6, 1898, Gwynn, 1929: 1: p. 196.

[19] Spring Rice to Roosevelt, Oct. 17, 1899, Roosevelt Papers.

[20] Roosevelt to Spring Rice, Dec. 2, 1899, *Roosevelt Letters* 2: p. 1103.

[21] Roosevelt to Lee, Dec. 13, 1899, Lee Papers; see also Roosevelt to Spring Rice, July 3, 1901, *Roosevelt Letters* 3: p. 109.

[22] Roosevelt to Lee, Dec. 13, 1899, Lee Papers.

[23] For example, Lee to Roosevelt, Jan. 29, 1900, Roosevelt Papers: also Strachey to Roosevelt, Feb. 1, 1900, *ibid.*

Your civil war is very much in our mind and we are able to draw inspiration from the way in which through weary years of discouragement you stuck to your guns. And how like the Boer oligarchy is the Southern slave-owning oligarchy. Just the same virtues and patriotism and the same haughty resolve not to share power with those they despise and dislike.[24]

Roosevelt was certain the British had to treat the Boers fairly, and he managed to see still other analogies with the American Civil War history in the South African conflict. "Do you think that in a short time it would be well to grant complete amnesty to the Cape Colony insurgents?" he inquired of Strachey. "After the well nigh intolerable strain of our Civil War it was done, although the leaders of the Confederation had been in the United States military service. The granting of suffrage is another matter, at least for the present," he continued; "although as you know, even the suffrage was not long withheld after our Civil War. But it does seem to me that it is the policy of both wisdom and of mercy steadily to grant a universal amnesty; excepting only such specified individuals as have, for grave reasons, to be taken out."[25] Were all this accomplished, in Roosevelt's judgment, the country would become "an English-speaking commonwealth like Australia, where the descendents of the Englishman and the Dutchman will live side by side, gradually growing indistinguishable from one another until they become fused just exactly as they have become in the United States."[26] The ultimate reason for TR's confidence in the future was a matter of race. He wrote Strachey of meeting a group of Boer prisoners of war passing through the United States on the way from Bermuda to their South African homes.

They are a fine set of men, admirable stock out of which to make a nation . . . in all fundamentals exactly like a set of our northern or western backwoods farmers, or the survivors among your yeomen and small farmers in the wilder or rougher parts of England. . . . I am certain that the Boer farmer can become part of an English-speaking, homogeneous population of mixed origins, which will not only make South Africa an important country but a very valuable addition to the English-speaking stock throughout the world.[27]

The Roosevelt circle of friends also placed the Boer War in the larger framework of contemporary world politics. One of Britain's fears was foreign intervention in the war, perhaps inspired by Germany.[28] Strachey spoke this fear to Roosevelt in early 1900, even though his best judgment tended to see Germany as a continental European power and not a colonial one.

Alluding also to the possibility of German penetration of Latin America, he told TR that he offered his ideas "as a friend of America."[29] In assessing the impact of the South African war on world politics Roosevelt was more direct. "If the British Empire suffer a serious disaster [as defeat in the Boer War] I believe in five years it will mean a war between us and some one of the great continental European military nations, unless we are content to abandon our Monroe Doctrine for South America," he predicted to Arthur Lee.[30] Given such comments evidently the Anglo-Americans realized that something more than Dutch independence vs. British hegemony in South Africa was involved in the outcome of the war. The world balance of power and the possible fate of the English-speaking peoples were in question. Partly because of such considerations and partly because Great Britain proceeded to treat the defeated Boers honorably, British popularity in the United States, which had sagged badly as the Boers heroically resisted conquest, quickly recovered with the peace.[31]

The construction of an Isthmian canal was both an important element in the world balance of power and an event which helped to define more precisely the character of the developing Anglo-American special relationship. For a time the canal proposal caused real friction between London and Washington, but its peaceful resolution came to be looked upon by both nations as further evidence that they should and could compose their particular differences for the sake of their broader common interest. At the end of the nineteenth century American expansionists were anxious to build a canal somewhere across Central America, and negotiations were undertaken with Great Britain for a new treaty which would supersede the Clayton-Bulwer Treaty of 1850, thereby erasing the prohibition on exclusive United States control of the proposed waterway. For Americans the crucial condition of the canal soon became the right of the United States to fortify it once it was built. Britain preferred a neutral canal and, when the first Hay-Pauncefote Convention (1900) was drawn up, a furor broke out in America over that provision stipulating a neutral waterway. Theodore Roosevelt was one of the most vigorous and outspoken proponents of an American canal, fully fortified to protect United States interests, and was therefore antagonistic to the official position of the British government.

Great Britain yielded but slowly to the persuasions of American power on the Isthmian canal controversy. But in private at least one of Roosevelt's English friends was disposed to favor a fortified United States canal from the outset, recognizing it as part of Anglo-

24 *Ibid.*

25 Roosevelt to Strachey, June 20, 1902, Strachey Papers.

26 Roosevelt to Spring Rice, Jan. 27, 1900, *Roosevelt Letters* 2: p. 1146; Roosevelt to Spring Rice, March 2, 1900, *ibid.* 2: p. 1209.

27 Roosevelt to Starchey, July 18, 1902, Strachey Papers.

28 Strachey to Roosevelt, Feb. 1, 1900, Roosevelt Papers; see also Roosevelt to Spring Rice, March 12, 1900, *Roosevelt Letters* 2: p. 1216.

29 Strachey to Roosevelt, Feb. 1, 1900, Roosevelt Papers.

30 Roosevelt to Lee, Jan. 30, 1900, *Roosevelt Letters* 2: p. 1152.

31 Both Strachey and Lee spoke their concern over loss of public friendliness in the United States during the war; see Strachey to Roosevelt, Feb., 1, 1900, Roosevelt Papers; Lee to Roosevelt, Jan. 29, 1900, *ibid.*

American cooperation in the world. About the time of the Yonkers Conference (February, 1900) which Roosevelt participated in and which issued a strongly worded memorandum insisting on United States control over the canal in peace and in war, St. Loe Strachey wrote TR:

I am very glad about the canal. That will greatly increase your Naval Power if war comes over South America and you can combine your Pacific and Atlantic Squadrons at pleasure while Germany can't. I don't believe the stories about our government stipulating against fortifications. That would be too idiotic even for our Foreign Office.

In Strachey's mind there was no issue at all. "You will of course fortify it [the canal] and if and when you like by means of coast defense vessels which can land their guns when wanted." [32] Strachey took the same tack in the columns on the *Spectator,* a fact which Roosevelt appreciated. TR explained himself to Spring Rice.

As the *Spectator* said, it is really for England's interest that America fortify the canal. Of course from our standpoint I think that in the event of our having trouble with Germany or France it would be far better not to have the canal at all than to have it unfortified and if we give Germany and France the right to come in on the Canal I fail to see how we could keep them out if they wanted to divide Brazil. [33]

Months later, with the issue still undisposed of, Roosevelt and Strachey continued to fret. From Cairo Strachey wrote:

I have always thought the second Hay Treaty as being sound and helpful from the American point of view—a piece of grand diplomatic work which will save many diplomatic worries and questions (not with us but with the rest of the world) and give America in fact though not in name complete control of the Canal. Still if America insists and does not mind the possibilities of friction that would arise from a specific right to fortify and non-neutralize, I can not see why we should mind. I can only speak for myself and I should not be surprized to hear our Foreign Office quite petrified on the subject. [34]

Roosevelt returned a remarkably similar letter, appealing to Strachey's Anglo-Americanism.

There is a very genuine desire to see the Canal in American hands. This is not aimed at Great Britain, because Great Britain is the one power which in the event of war with one of the continental powers whose fleet is approximately of the force of our own, it would be in the judgment of many most undesirable to have the canal open, while on the other hand, if it were in our possession it would add to our strength. [35]

At this juncture, however, it was not Strachey who was unconvinced but the British government, as Roosevelt's exchange with Arthur Lee so well showed.

Though he favored an American-built canal in Central America, Arthur Lee had reservations about its fortification by the United States. He took a firm line on this issue in his letters to Roosevelt, partly because he felt that any sort of meaningful Anglo-American accord had to be grounded on mutual respect. In January, 1901, when the outcome of the controversy was still far from certain, he wrote his friend of his misgivings. "Personally I have no objection whatever to a mutual abrogation of the Clayton-Bulwer Treaty, and see no possible harm to us (or advantage to the U.S.!) in the Senate's amendments." But what of the bad effects likely to be produced?

The great question is, would it be good policy for England to make any further concessions to that section of American feeling represented by the majority of the Senate. Would it perhaps develop hatred into contempt and encourage the cry that England is afraid and has no choice but to submit when America cracks the whip? . . . I think there may be real danger in too much complaisance. [36]

Roosevelt was not moved. Responding to Lee, he assured him that full United States control of the proposed waterway was not anti-British at all but grew out of the hard facts of national security. He went on to warn that the Senate, like himself, would not yield the point. "It does not seem to me that the amendments give any specific ground for grievance in Great Britain; and very many men on this side, men who are entirely friendly to England, feel that the amendments represent the utmost possible in the way of concessions from us." Further, he told Lee, the Senate's rejection of the first Hay-Pauncefote agreement was in no way a case of "bad faith." "Remember that no treaty is binding until the Senate has confirmed it," he chided his friend. All of which led Roosevelt to state unequivocally his own convictions regarding national self-interest.

The question is purely one as to the wisdom or unwisdom of the action sought. Similarly, in my judgment, the nation has as a matter of course a right to abrogate a treaty in solemn and formal manner for what she regards as sufficient cause, just exactly as she has a right to declare war or to exercise any other power for sufficient cause. [37]

Undismayed by Roosevelt's *machtpolitik,* Lee reasserted his position on a neutral canal even more forcefully in a letter dated April 2, 1901. To him the canal controversy was "one of the most awkward fences along the whole course" of Anglo-American friendship, to be taken successfully if the two nations proceeded "steadily and not try to rush it." Lee admitted that the question in the United States was "a great national question—here it is only a side issue involving a point of principle. But the latter is more a definite point than perhaps you realize," he observed. "I can not too strongly assure

---

[32] Strachey to Roosevelt, Feb. 1, 1900, *ibid.*
[33] Roosevelt to Spring Rice, March 2, 1900, *Roosevelt Letters* 2: p. 1208.
[34] Strachey to Roosevelt, Dec. 5, 1900, Roosevelt Papers.
[35] Roosevelt to Starchey, March 8, 1901, *Roosevelt Letters* 3: p. 9.

[36] Lee to Roosevelt, Jan. 25, 1901, Roosevelt Papers.
[37] Roosevelt to Lee, March 18, 1901, *Roosevelt Letters* 3: p. 19.

you that there is every desire here that the Canal should be built and administered by the United States for their exclusive profit, so long as the status of neutrality is not interfered with." This neutrality provision, Lee reminded his friend, had been part of the Clayton-Bulwer understanding as well as the first Hay-Pauncefote convention.[38] Lee then stated the British case without equivocation and with a good deal of authority.

... the negotiations assume the following aspect from our point of view.

And in saying this I have the highest authority for saying that this *is* the view of the British cabinet on the subject.

Perhaps the most powerful statesman we have said to me only this afternoon:

"Our view of the case is this. A comes to B and says: 'You have certain contract rights which are very inconvenient to my business, and I want you to forego them.' B does not want to at all but out of pure friendliness says: 'Very well, I am anxious to oblige,' and actually agrees to every request as proposed by A. Some time after, A re-appears and says:—'I have partners in my business—and they are not satisfied, and insist that you abandon all your control and rights. In fact, they state that they have cancelled our firm's signature to the original contract, and request that you will ratify this action on their part. At the same time it is pretty clearly indicated—through unofficial but important channels—that if B doesn't accept this 'trouble will follow.'

(It must be also added that in *this* instance B is a proud and powerful nation which has very recently given signal proof of its friendship to A and is no 'little state' that has no alternative but to submit!)

To this revised proposition B replies:—'I am very sorry that I can not accede to these last fresh demands, although I have clearly shown my desire to assist your plans by accepting everyone of your original proposals. For the present, therefore, we return to the 'status quo', until we can arrive at some better understanding."

So much for my parable—which, as I have said, originates from a very high source; and which, rightly or wrongly, represents very clearly and forcibly the British point of view.[39]

This position, adhered to for so many months by the London government, illustrated the source of the difficulty in attaining an entente between Great Britain and the United States. Not until British statesmen had become more fully convinced of the advantages of Anglo-American accord, purchasable at the price of defeat on an important if specific issue like a fortified canal, would they be inclined to give way. In so doing they sacrificed what they considered a treaty right and, if Lee was correct, a principle also, in pursuit of their broader national interest in a world that now included the United States as a great and potentially friendly power.

While negotiations were still stalemated Lee told Roosevelt he was convinced that there must be time for

a calm reconsideration of the whole matter, and . . . that diplomacy and good temper may succeed in framing a new

treaty sufficiently tactful to pacify the Senate. Meanwhile the less said in public about the treaty the better, and if I see any fear of the matter coming up in our Parliament here I shall use every kind of 'blocking' device to stave off discussion. This is, I think, the best service *I* can render!

And he continued:

Personally, I believe that the best chance for the new treaty would lie in extreme simplicity. In colloquial form, I would suggest merely the following. "We agree to cancel the Clayton-Bulwer treaty, merely reaffirming that the Canal when built shall always be neutral, and open to commerce of all nations and the world.

There should be no complicated provisions for peace or war. These merely incite controversy; and every one knows that in case of war, or real national danger, treaties become waste paper and each nation does what it thinks necessary for its own interests. Moreover all the treaties and fortifications in the world would not be able to keep the canal open to the passage of warships in wartime—so such provisions in a treaty are merely useless invitations to controversy and disagreements.

In short if the U.S. propose to England a simple guarantee of neutrality—I believe the only obstacle to the building of the canal—as far as we are concerned—will be for ever removed.[40]

Roosevelt was unimpressed, judging from his reply of April 24, 1901:

I have read your letter over very carefully, and it seems to me, if you will let me say so, old man, that you justify my position when you write as follows: "Everyone knows that in case of war or real national danger, treaties become as waste paper, and each nation does what it thinks necessary for its own interests. . . ." Yet you say in your opinion the treaty should declare that the "canal when built shall be *always neutral*, and open to the commerce of the world." Now, I am no diplomat, and of course I agree with you absolutely that no nation can be perpetually bound, to its own destruction, by a treaty. But it seems to me that this is very different from entering into a treaty with the intention that it shall be treated as wastepaper in certain contingencies. In the treaty as actually proposed either we meant what we said, or we did not. . . . I felt that it would be criminal in this nation to allow the canal to be used against it in time of war, or not to use the canal in its own interests during such a crisis. As I have said before, this consideration in my mind did not apply to England at all. England's navy would render it absolutely certain that whether the canal was fortified or not, and no matter what treaty stipulation should exist, it would immediately fall into her hands in case there was a war between England and the United States. As a matter of fact, if the possibility of war between England and the United States were all there was to consider, it would be wholly to the advantage of the United States to have outside powers guarantee the neutrality of the canal in time of war. But in the event of war with any power of continental Europe, I have felt that such neutrality would be a great disadvantage to our country. . . . In any case why say that the canal shall always be neutral when you yourself explicitly state that in making this promise neither side would have the slightest intention of abiding by it the minute it became its interest to break it. . . .[41]

[38] Lee to Roosevelt, April 2, 1901, Roosevelt Papers.
[39] *Ibid.* (Italics in original.)

[40] *Ibid.*
[41] Roosevelt to Lee, April 24, 1901, *Roosevelt Letters* 3, p. 65. (Italics in original.)

As this exchange of points of view demonstrated, the national interest of their respective countries was uppermost in the minds of Roosevelt and his English counterpart.

With the altering circumstances of increased United States commitment in the Caribbean and in hemispheric politics generally, the meaning of the Monroe Doctrine in Anglo-American relations inevitably came to the fore. Certain English newspapers, including the *Times,* voiced alarm that America's growing power was inimical to British interests in the New World and feared that the Monroe Doctrine might be invoked against England. Writing to Spring Rice in July, 1901, Roosevelt denied that any such possible implication was in his mind. "As things are now, the Monroe Doctrine does not touch England in any shape or way, and that the only power that needs to be reminded of its existence is Germany."[42] The fact is that Roosevelt was anxious to have the United States and Great Britain friendly, and at the same time to have an American canal on American terms. Arthur Lee discussed the application of the Monroe Doctrine, once the Senate had approved the canal treaty in December, 1901. Lee was faced with a complete American diplomatic victory. Desirous of putting what had happened in the best possible light, at the same time he wished to explain to Roosevelt, who was by that date president, how he assessed the future relations of the United States and England in the western hemisphere. These and other matters he took up in a long letter, dated December 17, 1901.

I hardly need tell you how delighted I was to see this morning that the much debated Canal Treaty had weathered all opposition, and had been ratified by the Senate by such an overwhelming majority. The smooth success of the Treaty has been very near my heart, and it has been my earnest desire all along to do any little thing that I could to remove any of the earlier difficulties that existed upon this side of the water.

The passage of the canal treaty, before the meeting of Parliament, Lee explained, had relieved him from the necessity of defending it in the House of Commons. He then continued:

It is likely however if an opportunity arises of discussing Anglo-American relations that I shall speak in favor of a formal recognition of the Monroe Doctrine by our government. The only thing that is at all doubtful, in my opinion, about this is whether such a recognition would be particularly gratifying or acceptable to the American people, but I have no doubt whatever that it would be for the best interests of the British Empire. It would not of course increase our popularity in Europe, but I hope, we shall never waste much time angling for that, and it would suggest to foreigners a large measure of common understanding between the two great sections of the English speaking peoples. That would be the most effective safe-guard that could be devised for the peaceful development of those peoples.[43]

Roosevelt's reply to Lee closed serious discussion of the Canal issue.

I suppose that in my present position I have no business to put down on paper even to as close a friend as you are, all I should like to say, for one can never tell when a letter will by accident get into some one else's hand—and there are such an infinite number of fools in the world. . . . But I must say how pleased I was by the ratification of the treaty. Really I think it is as much to your interest as to ours.[44]

A sense of intimacy and warm understanding, even a vague uneasiness over victory won at the expense of a friend, perhaps all of this was the president's way of reassuring Lee about the prospects of Anglo-American solidarity.

Roosevelt's assurances were far from gratuitous, for concurrently with the canal controversy the long simmering feud between Canada and the United States over the Alaskan boundary was troubling relations in both London and Washington. Discovery of gold in the Klondike in 1896 had made a determination of a boundary between American and Canadian territory imperative. By the time Theodore Roosevelt became president, the controversy had gone through a number of phases. A joint Canadian-American High Commission in 1898 had been unable to draw a mutually acceptable boundary line; a plan by Secretary of State Hay and Ambassador Choate for true arbitration of the matter ran afoul Canadian domestic politics. Meanwhile a *modus vivendi* worked out by Hay in October, 1899, which was largely favorable to the United States governed the situation. Hay had already commenced negotiations to replace this expedient arrangement with a permanent solution by means of a bi-national commission—a proposal rejected by Canada—before TR assumed office. Nor did the new president move on the issue directly. By his inaction he gave the *modus vivendi,* which he had objected to when it was originated, his tacit approval. When the Canadians thus rejected Hay's proposal for a bi-national commission in favor of true arbitration, Roosevelt reacted strongly. "I feel a good deal like telling them that if trouble comes it will be purely because of their own fault and although it would not be pleasant for us, it would be death for them," the president complained to Arthur Lee.[45] By early 1903 the London government, anxious for an amicable settlement irrespective of local Canadian advantage, agreed to a new American proposal for an even numbered Arbitration Commission of "six impartial jurists of repute," three from each side. The issue was ready to move off dead center where it had been so long anchored.

The Alaska boundary matter first claimed the attention of Roosevelt and his English correspondents in the spring of 1901 in an exchange between Arthur Lee and TR. Roosevelt, who was then vice-president, likened

[42] Roosevelt to Spring Rice, July 3, 1901, *ibid.* 3: p. 109.
[43] Lee to Roosevelt, Dec. 17, 1901, Roosevelt Papers.

[44] Roosevelt to Lee, Dec. 31, 1901, *Roosevelt Letters* 3: p. 224.
[45] Roosevelt to Lee, April 24, 1903, *ibid.* 3: p. 66.

the attitude of England toward a canal treaty favorable to the United States with "the Alaska boundary business." The American assumed a firm position.

I have studied that question pretty thoroughly and I do not think the Canadians have a leg to stand on. We might just as well claim part of New Foundland as to allow for one moment the Canadian claim to go to any point within ten miles of navigable water in Alaska. I do not know that anything more can be accomplished by treaty. At least I hope that nothing will happen which will tend to check the slow but on the whole steady growth of good feeling between the countries as it has been checked in the last few month.[46]

Lee's rejoinder was no less direct:

And now—as you have raised the question in your letter— I must say a few words about the Alaska Boundary Question, from *our* point of view. Personally I do not pretend to form a definite opinion as to the merits of the Canadian case, as although I have been to Alaska, and studied the maps on the spot, I do not feel qualified to pronounce judgment.

At the same time I do not by any means doubt that the US are in the right; but it must not be forgotten that Canada also claims and thinks *she* is in the right! And all England suggests in the matter is that the Canadian contention should be seriously investigated by impartial judges.

It is here necessary to remember that in 1895–96 there was a boundary dispute between England and Venezuela. England thought she was right, while Venezuela was equally confident of the justice of *her* case. Whereupon the US intervenes (with some aggressiveness!) and *insists* that England shall submit the whole dispute to arbitration.

England agrees, and the consequent proceedings vindicate her claims.

Now, another boundary dispute arises, with the US as one of the parties concerned. England, mindful of the precedent of 1895–96, suggests arbitration.

But the US refuses—and say in effect "oh—no—we won't arbitrate about the boundary because Canada 'haven't a leg to stand upon.'" But (setting aside the inability of one party to a dispute deciding this point) *if* the American case is so overwhelmingly sound why not accept arbitration, and so demonstrate the soundness of your claims before the world?

This would follow precedent laid down by yourselves and silence all comment. But in refusing to arbitrate you naturally invite the comment that the US policy only approve of arbitration when it can not possibly affect their own interests! Besides which there is no doubt that the inconsistent attitude of the US in this matter, and the bald plan of "non possumus" has caused a certain amount of irritation in English official circles, and may make our government less ready to make concessions to the US in other matters of dispute.

Lee's deep anxiety over Alaska was evident as he further explored the issue:

Of course I know what sort of a jingo answer the Senate and the Press would make to this statement; but forget that you are an American for a moment, and put yourself in our place and say if our view of the matter is not natural and reasonable!

I firmly believe that England is always willing to go further in the way of concession and friendly service to

the US than to all other nations of the earth combined, but it can not be "all give and no take," and your people should remember that we also are very proud and very powerful.[47]

A week later, fearing that he had spoken too bluntly, Lee sent TR an apology. He said he felt that he could write as he had because Roosevelt was a valued friend, concluding that he had no wish to draw the vice-president into controversy.[48]

The argument between the two friends, as between the two nations, had been fairly joined as was evident in TR's reply, dated April 24, 1901. He began by advising Lee that he was in no way speaking as an official of the McKinley administration in stating his views, that his letter was "purely personal both as coming from me, and as going to you." As for Alaska,

My own horseback judgment is (and it is mere horseback judgment liable to be upset) that we might as well let the *modus vivendi* be. By this *nodus vivendi* we give you a bit of territory to which as I firmly believe you have no more right than we have to take part of Cornwall or Kent. But so highly do I esteem the friendly relations with Great Britain that I should be willing to make the sacrifice by simply continuing the *modus vivendi*. I doubt if we could embody the matter in a treaty, simply because I think it would be a naked giving away of our territory to your people—a surrender which would be impossible to justify. But the territory to which I allude is of small value, and I think, judging from such information as I have that it would be best when we have reached a settlement not to disturb it—always providing that it is possible to let the *modus vivendi* stand. You ask why we should not arbitrate? My answer is simply that there are cases where a nation has no business to arbitrate. This Canadian claim to the disputed territory in Alaska is entirely modern. Twenty years ago the Canadian maps showed the lines just as ours did. They have no such *prima facie* case as the Venezuelans had. You did not arbitrate the Transvaal matter, and I do not see very well how you could have arbitrated it; so I do not with my present knowledge and feelings see how we could arbitrate about Alaska, except in some form of coming to an agreement among ourselves.

I hope you will come here this year. We want to see you both very much.

Roosevelt's letter included the following handwritten postscript:

It is hard to get *any* treaty through the Senate. There is always sure to be a considerable minority anxious to reject it so as to embarrass the administration; and a smaller minority anxious to do anything against England. With those two elements in view, I want to be dead sure a treaty is all right before making an effort to get it through.[49]

Lee again took up the boundary matter with Roosevelt after the latter had become president. Under these altered circumstances Lee's tone evinced moderation, but his purpose was not to mollify the chief executive

[46] Roosevelt to Lee, March 18, 1901, *ibid.* 3: p. 20.

[47] Lee to Roosevelt, April 2, 1901, Roosevelt Papers. (Italics in original.)
[48] Lee to Roosevelt, April 11, 1901, Lee Papers.
[49] Roosevelt to Lee, April 24, 1901, *Roosevelt Letters* 3: pp. 65–66.

so much as it was to discuss another aspect of the problem, emphasizing to Roosevelt just how awkward the British position had become.

> The only possible cloud that I see ahead on the Anglo-American horizon is the Alaska Boundary Question, and I do earnestly hope that it may be found possible to let sleeping dogs lie and to leave the "modus vivendi" undisturbed as long as possible. If this question does come up it will not be of our seeking here in England, but will be forced upon us by Canada. It is often said that in the case we have merely to snub Canada, and I must confess that from my five years experience of that country I should not be very adverse to doing so, but I feel sure that you will recognize the extreme difficulty of our position as regards Canadian wishes. During the last decade Canada has set an example to the rest of the Empire in matters of practical patriotism, and even at this moment is making fresh sacrifices to show her complete loyalty to our cause in South Africa. Under these circumstances it would be difficult to snub her, even if we thought it best to do so, but the English people have to be reckoned with, and in their present feeling of gratitude towards the Colonies they would vigorously resent any action which could be construed into a neglect of Colonial interests.[50]

The issue remained stalemated nonetheless. Roosevelt was determined to maintain what he saw as American national interests. He made these same representations to St. Loe Strachey in July, 1902, as the Arbitration Agreement was being negotiated.

> Just at the moment in my relations with Great Britain I am suffering from anxiety. I do not think the Canadians have a leg to stand on in the Alaska boundary dispute; and this being the case, I do not see how I can assent to any compromise. And yet I thoroughly understand how the English in the moment of victory, when the Canadians as well as the citizens of the other colonial commonwealths have stood by them so loyally, feel that they must stand by the Canadians in return.[51]

At this point in the disagreement even Strachey took exception to the American stand. To him the boundary dispute was a "kind of night-mare." "I see of course your objection to arbitration," he wrote,

> but I also see what a terrible position it will put us in here if you refuse and especially people like me who insisted that the American demand for arbitration in the case of Venezuela must be yielded to. However, when I am most pessimistic over this wretched boundary dispute I remember that you are president of the United States and that Balfour is our prime minister and I know that both of you will count your political lives failures if war should come between the two English speaking nations in your time.[52]

To such pleas the president made no concessions.

President Roosevelt's appointment of the American members of the Arbitration Commission—Henry Cabot Lodge, Elihu Root, and George Turner, men who had small claim to being "impartial jurists of repute"— brought him much criticism. In the judgment of

Arthur Lee these appointments violated the whole spirit of the agreement to arbitrate.[53] TR may have been stung by his friend's strictures for he wrote at some length to Lee defending his action.

> Now as to Alaska: Have you seen the maps in the big red atlas prepared by the British commissioners, and on the outside printed "British Case"? If so, I want you to take what the British Commission—that is, the two Canadian Commissioners and Lord Alverstone—submitted in the way of maps, and note that every Canadian and British map thus officially submitted by the British and Canadian Commissioners, for sixty years after the signing of the treaty between the Russians and the British in 1825, sustained the American case. Lord Alverstone could not have decided otherwise than he did, and the action of the Canadian Commissioners, in my view, was outrageous alike from the standpoint of ethics and of professional decency. There is nothing I should enjoy more than to write an article about Lord Alverstone, reproducing all these maps, so that even the least thoughtful could see that Lord Alverstone could not, as an honorable man, decide otherwise than he did; and that as a matter of fact, he got every inch of territory for the Canadians that could by any possibility be held to be theirs. The only reason I do not say somthing in public in the matter is that I am afraid it might do Lord Alverstone hurt instead of good, but you are very welcome to show him this letter if you see fit.
>
> You speak of your regret that the Commission was not composed exclusively of judges. I asked two judges of our Supreme Court, whom I thought most fit for the positions, to serve. They both declined, and as I now think, wisely. On this Commission we needed to have jurists who were statesmen. If the decision had been rendered purely judicially, *the Canadians would not have received the two islands which they did receive at the mouth of the Portland Canal;* and one of the judges to whom I offered the appointment has told me that on that account he would not have been able to sign the award. He would have felt that he was sitting purely as a judge, and that judicially the case did not admit of compromise. . . . My belief is that if you had had two of our Supreme Court judges on the American Commission, they would have stood out steadily for a decision on every point in favor of the American view—a determination that would have been technically proper, but in its results most unfortunate.[54]

About the same time Roosevelt made a similar defense of his policy and its outcome, which was almost wholly favorable to the United States, in a letter to Spring Rice.

> If you get here I want to show you the maps submitted by the British Commission to the Alaska boundary case. These maps, to my mind, show exclusively that there was literally no Canadian case at all on their main points, and that the Canadian Commissioners are inexcusably attacking Lord Alverstone [55] as they have done. He could not have done otherwise. On points where there was room for genuine controversy there was, as there should have been, give and take between him and the American Commissioners; but on the points raised by the Canadians there was really no room for controversy whatever.

[50] Lee to Roosevelt, Dec. 17, 1901, Roosevelt Papers.
[51] Roosevelt to Strachey, July 18, 1902, Strachey Papers.
[52] Strachey to Roosevelt, Aug. 18, 1902, Roosevelt Papers.

[53] Lee to Roosevelt, Nov. 22, 1903, *ibid.*
[54] Roosevelt to Lee, Dec. 7, 1903, *Roosevelt Letters* 3: p. 665. (Italics in original.)
[55] Lord Alverstone, British judge on the Commission.

And TR added by way of conclusion: "It has been a very fortunate and happy thing to get the question definitely settled and out of the way," which, understandably, was the way he preferred his English friends to remember the episode.[56]

In both canal diplomacy and the Alaska boundary question Great Britain came to know the determination of Theodore Roosevelt to satisfy American national interest, even if it brought discomfort to the English. Because of his Anglo-Americanism he did not allow disagreement to become detachment, however. Assessing United States policy, the London government had some better understanding of what the Anglo-American entente meant in reality as opposed to the realm of sentiment. In the negotiations leading to the Treaty of Portsmouth, which brought the Russo-Japanese War to a peaceful end, Roosevelt experienced a similar sense of national interest, as the British conceived their own to be, in Downing Street's refusal to facilitate Roosevelt's efforts to conclude the conflict. Great Britain as an ally of Japan since 1902 was in a position to exert some pressure on her Asian friend, had she looked upon this as strengthening her hand in world politics. On the contrary, the British for a long while hoped for a sweeping Japanese victory, judging this as the way best designed to meet her own needs in the Orient. Roosevelt preferred to balance an emerging Japan against an established Russia, partly because he feared an all-powerful Japan as a threat to the United States in the Far East. As a result of this diverging appreciation of the implications inherent in the war—at first Washington as well as London favored a decisive Japanese victory—TR received limited British encouragement, particularly as it appeared that Japan would win.[57] When, after a series of stunning triumphs over Russia in 1904 and 1905, the Japanese nonetheless found themselves facing bankruptcy, Britain was somewhat more disposed to support Roosevelt's peace enterprise. In the late winter of 1904–1905, for example, before the battle of Tsushima (May 27, 1905) which ravaged the Russian fleet, Spring Rice came to Washington to act as a special intermediary between Lord Lansdowne and the president. But there was no meeting of the Anglo-American minds. Shortly thereafter Britain ceased to second Roosevelt's moves toward mediation. By summer this posture had altered. Spring Rice wrote the president in July:

The object of England is to see peace established. Lord Lansdowne in reading your words repeated the phrase: "I hope the English people will use their influence *at the proper time* to prevent the Japanese from asking impossible terms. He thinks the "proper time" may come

when and if it is apparent that Japan is insisting on impossible terms which make peace impossible. Up to the present moment he has no information which points to this. The moment may come. When it does come, he hopes the American government may communicate with him with absolute frankness. They can be quite sure that their views will receive the fullest and friendliest consideration.[58]

The very next month Spring Rice informed the president, by enclosing a letter that Lansdowne had written to him, that the foreign minister strongly supported TR's role as peacemaker and that it was London's view that it was to Japan's best interest to get out of the war quickly.[59]

Despite disagreement over the timing of Russo-Japanese peace talks—a difference of opinion lasting several months—no falling out between England and the United States occurred. Official channels of communication between the two governments did not completely dry up while semiofficial lines of communication remained constantly in use. Both of these considerations were illustrated by Roosevelt's comments to Arthur Lee in September, 1905, as the British were in the process of re-affirming their Japanese alliance. The president wrote:

I had been shown the rough draft of the Anglo-Japanese treaty before it was signed and expressed my hearty approval of it. I think it is a very good thing for England and Japan; and I think it is a decidedly good thing for the United States and the rest of the world for the reasons you gave. I have no patience with the people who clamor about its showing a "degenerate" condition in England. In my opinion it would show not only degeneration but ossification to refuse to recognize the growth and the power of Japan, and to make use of it when recognized.[60]

About the same time Roosevelt made similar comments to St. Loe Strachey:

As for Japan, all I can do to help her shall be done. It may be that we shall have trouble with her, and the attacks by the Tokio mob on foreigners and Christians have an ominous side, and tend to reconcile me to her failure to get a greater sum of money and to her being left face to face with Russia in Siberia, especially as the Anglo-Japanese alliance really guarantees her against any offensive return by Russia.[61]

To which Strachey replied: "Though it was impossible for you to bring the Japanese and the Russians together, you did it because you knew you had the order in your pocket—the order which a man feels when he has a true sense of duty." [62]

Roosevelt's casual letters to and from his English friends at the time of the Russo-Japanese War, as these touched on the conflict, were valuable for the sidelights thrown on the Anglo-American way of viewing

[56] Roosevelt to Spring Rice, Nov. 9, 1903, *Roosevelt Letters* 3: p. 650.

[57] For an interesting exchange on the subject of common Anglo-American action to end the war see Spring Rice to Roosevelt, Dec. 7, 1904, Gwynn, 1929: 1: pp. 438–440, and Roosevelt to Spring Rice, Dec. 27, 1904, *ibid.*, pp. 441–446.

[58] Spring Rice to Roosevelt, July 11, 1905, Roosevelt Papers. (Italics in original.)

[59] Spring Rice to Roosevelt, Aug. 8, 1905, Spring Rice Papers.

[60] Roosevelt to Lee, Sept. 21, 1905, Lee Papers.

[61] Roosevelt to Strachey, Sept. 11, 1905, Strachey Papers.

[62] Strachey to Roosevelt, Oct. 16, 1905, *ibid.*

the war. Their value was enhanced because of the strain on official diplomatic relations which diverging policies produced. During the course of the conflict and the peace talks the president's most faithful correspondent was Spring Rice, who was at the British Embassy in St. Petersburg when hostilities commenced in February, 1904. He wrote vivid descriptions of events to Edith Carow Roosevelt and arched political comments to Roosevelt himself.[63] Not unnaturally, Spring Rice's letters bore a pro-Japanese inflection. Japan and England were allies and his suspicions of Russia were deepgrained. This was how he explained the meaning of events to TR, with that air of cosmic finality that was his trade-mark.

I can't tell you how delightful it is to get such a letter from you and how glad I am to have such a friend. The world is not in very satisfactory condition and it is one firm pleasure at any rate to see a real man in the proper place for him, and to know that I know him.

I can't help thinking we are on the verge of great changes. What has happened here seems to be that the Emperor believed Japan was bluffing—was assured so by interested parties—and was encouraged by the war party and found it too late to retract. He absolutely refused to listen to his official councillor Lamsdorff and very often did not even tell him what had occurred.

Russia had been successful for many years in Asia in the policy of peaceful penetration—especially with England, who raised some ineffectual howls and ran; Japan had no question but one, that is Asia—and did not run. We spoiled Russia and she has to take the consequences. It is the firm conviction of Russia that the "Russian God" (an official expression) wills that Russia should occupy the whole of Asia; other nations are trespassers from overseas and have no rights. Treaties and engagements are temporary concessions in the weakness of the flesh, and must be got rid of when convenient. The point of view is that of a moral and religious right, supported by a feeling of innate conviction, and it is difficult to change. Japan was a mere trespasser in Corea, to be tolerated for a time and then removed. Treaty rights of foreigners were a temporary phase in the development of Asia which must disappear before the light of dawning Russia. This is no exaggeration, it is the general and universally received opinion. It is Russia's strength and this conviction exists and is acted on with all the force of the national conscience.

That Japan should have dared resist is inconceivable; that she attacked when Russia was not ready, was monstrous. The explanation is—England and America. These friends of Japan incited her against holy and just Russia: and they must pay and be punished. America is far off and rather tough. England has the juicy and succulent morsel (India) within reach. So England can be made to pay and must pay. If this were all it wouldn't be a very serious matter. I quite agree with what you always said: England is where Englishmen can breed English children—not where millions of black men, sweltering in the sun, admire, prostrate, an Imperial Viceroy. I could support the loss of India with equanimity, if it did not mean the loss of a great free market, as well as the destruction, and hopeless destruction, of the work of two centuries. But what is that in the East?[64]

Since the diplomacy of the United States and Great Britain did not converge until the late summer of 1905 the letters that passed between Roosevelt and his friends tended either toward the ultimate dispositions, as in the foregoing generalities, or to personalities. The president informed Spring Rice, for example, that he was sending "a close friend of mine," George Meyer, as American ambassador to Russia. After Meyer's arrival Spring Rice replied: "Meyer is come and is very much liked. He seems to have a very level head and will not be got at by the Grand Dukes." [65] In a later letter Roosevelt gave Spring Rice his impressions of Count Witte. "Witte impressed me much while he was here, but by no means altogether pleasantly. He spoke with astonishing freedom of the hopeless character of Russian despotism. . . . I thought this pretty frank. . . . He also commented on the brutality of the treatment of political suspects with contempt and indignation." [66] Though their governments had been in some disagreement over policies, the semi-official lines of friendship, as between Roosevelt and Spring Rice, remained open and active.

Roosevelt was not unmindful that Britain could be of the very greatest help in bringing about a Far Eastern settlement. He wrote Spring Rice in late 1904:

It is always possible that Japan and Russia may come to terms of agreement. . . . My policy must of necessity be somewhat opportunist. . . . So far as this Eastern question is concerned I do not like to write my conclusions even to you. . . . I would hesitate in counting upon the support of your government and your people. I am not quite sure of their tenacity or fixity of purpose, of their willingness to take the necessary risks, and the need to endure heavy losses for a given goal.[67]

However, the president took occasion to reassure his English friends that at least his policies, aimed at bringing about peace, were not anti-British, though he did not choose to write all the details of his dealings with the Japanese. For example, in June, 1904, after writing to Spring Rice what must have seemed to be highly delicate information, he added solemnly: "Some of the things he [the Japanese minister] said I do not wish to put down on paper—which may astonish you in view of what I fear diplomatists would regard as the frankness of this letter anyhow." In a postscript he asserted an important point: "Don't misunderstand from the above that I was laying the ground for any kind of interference by this Government in the Far East. . . ." [68] In March of the following year Roosevelt told George O. Trevelyan that he had "privately and

---

[63] Spring Rice to Edith Carow Roosevelt, Feb., 1904, Gwynn, 1929: 1: p. 394; Spring Rice to Edith Carow Roosevelt, March 29, 1905, ibid., pp. 465–466.

[64] Spring Rice to Roosevelt, Feb. 1, 1904, ibid., 1: p. 394.

See also Roosevelt to Spring Rice, June 13, 1904, Roosevelt Letters 4: pp. 829–833.

[65] Roosevelt to Spring Rice, Dec. 27, 1904, ibid. 4: p. 1084; Spring Rice to Edith Carow Roosevelt, April 26, 1905, Roosevelt Papers.

[66] Roosevelt to Spring Rice, Nov. 1, 1905, ibid.

[67] Roosevelt to Spring Rice, Dec. 17, 1904, Roosevelt Letters 4: pp. 1084–1085.

[68] Roosevelt to Spring Rice, June 13, 1904, ibid. 4: p. 831.

unofficially advised the Russian Government and afterwards repeated the advice indirectly through the French Government, to make peace. . . ." [69] In June the president advised Spring Rice: "Well, it seems to me that the Russian bubble has been pretty thoroughly pricked." [70] Throughout these letters appeared little trace of resentment on the chief executive's part that the British had cooperated hardly at all to promote peace in the Orient. No doubt he did not write all that was on his mind, as his remark to Spring Rice suggested, and he spoke critically of the British attitude to others.[71] But even when the topic of differing policies did arise in the correspondence of Roosevelt and his friends, logic rather than rancor colored the president's arguments. At one time he chided Spring Rice about "needless heroics" respecting the contention that England's honor commanded her to abstain from persuading the Japanese to halt the war." [72] I wholly fail to understand the difference in position which makes it proper for France, the ally of Russia, to urge Russia to make peace and which yet makes it improper for England, the ally of Japan, to urge Japan . . . to make peace," TR contended in a letter to Spring Rice.[73] Roosevelt's willingness to take this tack may have been an indication of his desire not to alienate Great Britain at a time when he looked forward to her postwar support in handling matters of common concern in the Orient, as for example, a joint Anglo-American policy toward mass Japanese migrations to the United States and commonwealth countries of the Pacific.

Once serious peace negotiations were underway, a very friendly and congratulatory spirit prevailed on all sides. Inevitably the president sent a lengthy and detailed explanation of the proceedings to Spring Rice, including extracts of his correspondence with Baron Kaneko. A reply came to the president through Mrs. Roosevelt, supplying the American chief executive with informed but strongly opinionated views of how the peace talks looked from Petrograd. Spring Rice described what had happened by saying: "it is a fact beyond any question that the president single-handed effected a peace, against the wishes of the Japanese people and the Russian Government." [74] "I congratulate you a thousand times on the signature which bears a seal of great achievement," he wrote Roosevelt, once the Portsmouth Treaty had been signed.[75] The president also kept Strachey and Trevelyan informed of the peace talks.[76] Strachey replied:

I simply can not resist the temptation to tell you how proud and delighted I (like all your friends) was by your great triumph. I know you will value the personal triumph as less than nothing, but your friends have a right to rejoice in that as well as in the fact that you have given peace to the world. I feel sure that but for you, we should have had another year's war and with possible consequences that one does not care to contemplate.[77]

Such a comment usefully summarized the feelings of Roosevelt's English friends over the removal of an awkward disagreement between the two nations. Thereafter the Roosevelt circle had little or no occasion to divide over policy toward Japan. When the Root-Takahira Agreement was initialed in 1908 Lee called it a "real knock-out blow for the mischief mongers on both sides of the Atlantic." [78] All in all, Roosevelt responded to Lee, he believed his Japanese diplomacy "had borne good results." [79] In fact, however, at least one qualification of TR's evaluation must be indicated. This was the projected joint policy for restriction of Japanese immigrants to the English-speaking lands, that rimmed the Pacific. Here the president met a British rebuff, comparable in kind if not in magnitude to Roosevelt's hard line in the Alaska boundary dispute. Despite his maneuver to combine Canadian and American pressure on London, through the MacKenzie King mission, the London government resisted the offer of a joint policy against Japanese immigration. British interests called for a more cautious approach to Japan in order that the Anglo-Japanese alliance might be preserved.[80]

A less significant conflict of national interest between the United States and Great Britain developed out of the first Moroccan crisis of 1905, but in the end Anglo-American unity was strengthened by the episode. In arranging the Algeciras Conference for settling differences in North Africa between Germany and France, Great Britain's entente partner, President Roosevelt acted in good faith for peace. American concern in North Africa, political or economic, was negligible. The British, as allies of France, came to appreciate Roosevelt's role, and as potential foes of Germany welcomed his rebuff to German ambitions which the Conference produced. The president and Spring Rice

[69] Roosevelt to Trevelyan, March 9, 1905, *ibid.* 4: p. 1134.

[70] Roosevelt to Spring Rice, June 16, 1905, *ibid.* 4: p. 1233.

[71] For example, Roosevelt to Whitelaw Reid, Sept. 11, 1905, *ibid.* 5: pp. 18–20.

[72] Roosevelt to Spring Rice, July 24, 1905, *ibid.* 4: pp. 1283–1284.

[73] *Ibid.*, p. 1284.

[74] Spring Rice to Edith Carow Roosevelt, Sept. 26, 1905; Gwynn, 1929: 1: p. 490.

[75] Spring Rice to Edith Carow Roosevelt, Oct. 15, 1905, *ibid.* 1: p. 501.

[76] Roosevelt to Strachey, Sept. 11, 1905, Strachey Papers; see also Roosevelt to Trevelyan, Sept. 12, 1905, *Roosevelt Letters* 5: p. 22.

[77] Strachey to Roosevelt, Sept. 9, 1905, Roosevelt Papers.

[78] Lee to Roosevelt, Dec. 1, 1908, *ibid.*

[79] Roosevelt to Lee, Dec. 20, 1908, *Roosevelt Letters* 6: pp. 1432–1433.

[80] For a balanced judgment respecting Roosevelt, the MacKenzie King mission, and Japanese immigration, see Charles E. Neu, 1967: pp. 207–209 especially; Ian Nish, 1966; p. 340 speaks of the circumspect way in which the Foreign Office handled Japanese matters in so far as TR's knowledge was concerned. Raymond A. Esthus, 1967, is the best over-all treatment of Roosevelt and Japan.

shared their thoughts on the outcome of the meetings in the spring of 1905. Two letters from the White House assured Spring Rice that TR was not under the spell of the Kaiser in promoting the Conference. He went on to remark in one of the letters that he was sure that Germany had no "long settled and well thought out plans of attack on England, such as Bismarck developed first as regards Austria and then as regards France." In fact, he said, "I very sincerely wish I could get England and Germany into friendly relations." [81] Spring Rice remained suspicious. It is probable," he wrote,

that Germany will pursue her advantage and that in the Morocco Conference it will be made evident to the world and to the French people that France must yield or incur the imminent danger of a war with the support of a power that has not an equal stake in the struggle. For my part I shouldn't be sorry to see the English people convinced of the necessity of enduring great sacrifices in a good cause. We shall, I hope, take to heart your own words to your people that "we can only be saved by our own efforts and not by any alliance with anyone else.[82]

Fearful that Germany might somehow split the Anglo-French entente, which he considered important to world peace and stability, the president swung against the Germans at the Conference. However, his moves and maneuvering were clouded if not cloaked by the secrecy common to such negotiations so that many Englishmen became convinced of TR's hostility. His poor image in Britain was only temporary and he was completely rehabilitated by the outcome of the affair. In October, 1906, at a time when Lee was visiting him in Washington, he told Arthur Lee the details of his work at the Conference. As the facts slowly came to be understood by the British people at large, Lee was able to report: "I doubt if there is any responsible person left over here who harbours delusions any more about your alleged anti-British stance." [83] The promotion of peace and of Anglo-American solidarity had once more been demonstrated at Algeciras.

Theodore Roosevelt, the erstwhile warrior of the Spanish-American War, won the Nobel Prize for his peace efforts in ending the Russo-Japanese War. In this way, and in his work for international accord at the Algeciras Conference, he had become a vital force for peace. It was a style becoming to the era. The Hague Conferences of 1899 and 1907 and the London meeting in 1908 represented the concern, to a degree at least, of the Powers for the establishment of some sort of mechanism to settle disputes among nations without recourse to arms. Very often the advocates of international arbitration were looked upon as preferring "peace at any price." Roosevelt, who in his own way

had labored for peace both in the Orient and the Old World, insisted that, though he preferred war to surrender of national advantage, war for its own sake was pointless.[84] He explored the issue in writing to Spring Rice. "It is just as true now as ever it was in the old days that every free people must face the very difficult problem of combining liberal institutions and wide opportunities for happiness and well-being at home with power to make head against foreign foes." [85] And in another letter, to George Otto Trevelyan, TR came directly to the difficulty, warning that, if we should go too far in the way of arbitration, "we should put ourselves in the position of having the free peoples rendered helpless in the face of various military despotisms and barbarians in the world." [86] Roosevelt shared with certain of his English friends a suspicion of the "peace movements" as a possible threat to Anglo-American hegemony in the world. Giving serious thought to the "peace movements," Roosevelt observed to Strachey:

I need hardly repeat how earnestly I am for peace, but that I am for peace only when it is identical with justice —never when it is the alternative to justice. But it is a lamentable thing to see how many educated people whom civilization and education together have made anemic grow to shudder at whatever is really robust, and become fairly hysterical in denunciation of the manlier virtues . . . while it is also lamentable to see the way in which the hideous trait of regarding the achievement of wealth as the only legitimate end of ambition, tends to make the so-called successful man a man of nothing whatever but the money touch and therefore fit for nothing higher whether in war, politics, art, science or literature.[87]

Strachey's reply of complete agreement at the same time carried with it an assumption of Anglo-American superiority, whether in peace or war.[88] The editor of the *Spectator* made his point of the peculiar excellence of the English-speaking races more explicitly in a letter written to the president in 1907. He had just completed a tour of the continent during which he had visited all the major capital cities and had conversed with a great many political leaders. Anxious to give his impressions to Roosevelt of the various European statesmen he had met, he assumed the lofty attitude that while the German emperor "might be willing to engage in war for reasons of pure policy," to an English or American statesman such action would be "detestable." [89] Thus in so far as the Anglo-Americans were concerned, there was really no need for arbitration machinery to settle their differences, since both English and American leaders could be counted on to act honorably in their mutual dealings. Whether Strachey

[81] Roosevelt to Spring Rice, May 13, 1905, *Roosevelt Letters* 4: p. 1177. See also Roosevelt to Spring Rice, May 26, 1905, *ibid.*, p. 1194.

[82] Spring Rice to Roosevelt, July 11, 1905, Roosevelt Papers.

[83] Roosevelt to Lee, Oct. 15, 1906, Lee Papers; Lee to Roosevelt, March 28, 1907, Roosevelt Papers.

[84] Roosevelt to Strachey, Sept. 11, 1905, Strachey Papers.

[85] Roosevelt to Spring Rice, Dec. 27, 1904, *Roosevelt Letters* 4: p. 1083.

[86] Roosevelt to Trevelyan, Aug. 18, 1906, *ibid.* 5: p. 366.

[87] Roosevelt to Strachey, Sept. 7, 1906, Strachey Papers.

[88] Strachey to Roosevelt, Sept. 23, 1906, *ibid.*

[89] Strachey to Roosevelt, Feb. 11, 1907, Roosevelt Papers.

was moved to write this view because by 1907 most of the issues of dispute between his country and the United States had disappeared, or whether he spoke out of his feeling for the United States, both elements figured importantly in the increasingly smooth course of Anglo-American relations as Roosevelt's presidency came to a close. Because of such considerations, and quite apart from what other countries might or might not do, Strachey argued that "the two great free nations of the earth must think out some proper scheme under which they may combine safety with liberty."[90]

A comprehensive system of substantive arbitration among the great Powers was the bright hope of the movement for international peace down to the outbreak of World War I. Yet even kindred folk like the British and the Americans failed to agree on the use of this method to settle their vital differences, owing perhaps to the "immense capacity for resistance" on the part of the American Senate. The discussions of Roosevelt and his English friends surrounding arbitration, nonetheless, provided further opportunity to appraise the character of the maturing Anglo-American entente. While the Arbitration Treaty of 1911 was under consideration Ambassador Bryce, who favored such an agreement between his country and the United States, wrote to the ex-president:

There is not, as far as I can see, any reason why the one [arbitration agreement] it is hoped to make between you and us should be taken as a normal form to be employed between either of our countries and other countries. Personally I should not think that it would suit all cases. All sorts of things may do well between us and you which might not do well between ourselves and others.[91]

This same argument Strachey made with characteristic pungency, relating the problem directly to the need for military preparedness.

For myself, though I love the idea of a general arbitration treaty with the United States and believe it will do nothing but good, I am skeptical about general treaties with the world at large. Indeed, more humbug is talked about arbitration than any other subject in the world. . . . The world is not as Carnegie supposes a kind of gigantic Sunday School or Free Library, but instead a place of wild passions and fierce hostilities in which good men and good nations must move warily and well armed.[92]

In summary, both Bryce and Strachey took the view that it was the likenesses inherent in the two nations that rendered Anglo-American arbitration feasible, and by inference, the dissimilarities between them and other nations which made arbitration unworkable as a general rule.

Theodore Roosevelt tested the implications of Anglo-American cooperation in speaking his thoughts on arbitration to Arthur Lee. "Of course I personally would be willing and indeed anxious to make a very much closer arrangement with the British Empire than any other nation, or than is implied in any possible arbitration treaty . . . ," he wrote Lee. Yet the prospects, he judged, were limited by the facts; in his estimate "as yet neither nation is ready for such an arrangement."[93] A few weeks later he seemed to have adjusted his views, telling Lee: "If it [the arbitration treaty] were limited absolutely to England, well and good, but as a general model, to see such a treaty . . . as a model for treaties with all powers, I think would be poor business."[94] When Roosevelt was willing to come this far in support of Anglo-American arbitration both Lee and Strachey reciprocated warmly.[95] Still TR was uneasy over the prospects, for he believed deeply that the two English-speaking nations were separate sovereignties and this could not be dismissed as no longer relevant.[96] Roosevelt was too thoroughly an American to want to see his country in a situation where it might be required by treaty to arbitrate issues involving fundamental national interests. As he told Bryce, he did not believe he would agree to any treaty which would explicitly necessitate such action. To do so was "literally like a man solemnly covenanting that he will arbitrate being slapped in the face."[97] TR clearly preferred keeping a free hand, even relative to Great Britain, in the conviction that the Anglo-American special relationship could best be served by informal and genuine friendliness rather than formal and perhaps onerous commitments.

In the midst of their correspondence over the Arbitration Treaty, Roosevelt and Bryce pooled their thoughts on a permanent Anglo-American Union. "As regards the British Empire and the United States, I am a dreamer of dreams," the ex-president told Bryce.

I venture to hope that ultimately there may be some kind of intimate association between Great Britain and Ireland, Canada, Australia, South Africa, New Zealand and our own country, which will put us upon such a footing that we can literally have every question that may arise within our own limits settled exactly as similar difficulties within the British Empire or within the United States are now settled.[98]

Bryce's response was direct and optimistic.

The latter part of your letter where you refer to other possibilities as between the United States and the self-governing peoples comprised in the British Empire touches one of the largest and most interesting of all political questions. When you were President I was always hoping for an opportunity of discussing it with you; but you were

90 Strachey to Roosevelt, April 3, 1906, Strachey Papers.
91 Bryce to Roosevelt, June 10, 1911, Bryce Papers.
92 Strachey to Roosevelt, Oct. 27, 1911, Strachey Papers.

93 Roosevelt to Lee, June 27, 1911, Roosevelt Letters 7 : o. 296.
94 Roosevelt to Lee, Aug. 22, 1911, ibid. 7 : p. 338.
95 Lee to Roosevelt, Oct. 13, 1911, Lee Papers; see also Strachey to Roosevelt, Nov. 21, 1911, Strachey Papers.
96 Roosevelt once remarked to Lee that in Anglo-American relations he had an "11th commandment": "Thou shalt not slop over." Roosevelt to Lee, July 7, 1913, Roosevelt Letters 7 : p. 739.
97 Roosevelt to Bryce, June 2, 1911, ibid. 7 : p. 275.
98 Ibid.

incessantly busy and the moment never came. I hope it may come soon.[99]

This was the dominating spirit of Anglo-American relations down to the eve of the 1914 war, despite the rejection of the Arbitration Treaty itself. Not that Roosevelt and his friends always agreed on how that spirit should be translated into policy. As TR remarked to Arthur Lee respecting the abortive Canadian reciprocity treaty: "I was very reluctant to support it at all, and did so only as I should have supported any movement for closer relations with the British Empire in its entirety, or with the British Isles, Canada, or Australia, if I could not hope for closer relations with the Empire as a whole."[100]   On the subject of the Panama tolls dispute, which arose in 1912, Roosevelt told Lee that "Great Britain's position about coast-wise shipping is wrong," though he did admit the United States had to "fulfill without any quibble the spirit of the Panama Treaty."[101]   Later he was to say to Spring Rice that the Panama Question, which stemmed from congressional legislation exempting American coastal shipping from the payment of Canal tolls, should be arbitrated, even though he was lukewarm about the arbitration of such disputes.[102]   From the British side St. Loe Strachey referred to the spirit of friendship when he wrote of the tolls disagreement for the purpose of taking issue with the American attitude. Great Britain contended that the exemption of United States coastal shipping, as from New York to San Francisco, amounted to a discrimination in favor of American interests and in violation of the Canal treaty. "I fully realize," observed Strachey, "from one's experience of human affairs that although the thing looks plain as a pike-staff to me, other men may just as honestly and honourably hold the opposite view."[103]   James Bryce gave a proper Anglo-American interpretation of the tolls *contretemps*, explaining to Roosevelt as follows.

The thing is a small one in itself both for the United States and for us. What it does signify is that it should not cause misunderstanding or ill feeling. I am personally anxious that there should be no misconception in Europe of the attitude of the United States people, for no people seems more generally wishful to act fairly and rightly and observe its national obligations.[104]

The critical consideration for all the friends was that a spirit of friendship be maintained, so that if some fresh serious disagreement did arise good will from both sides would be ready to work out an acceptable accommodation.

IV. WAR

Anglo-American relations had never been better than they were in 1914, the year war broke out in Europe. The complications arising from that titanic struggle turned out to be an explicit test of the durability of the rapprochement, the eventual entry of the United States into the conflict in 1917 a cautious conformation to the pattern of Anglo-American affairs developed since 1898. The intersection of respective national interests which brought American military involvement was not inevitable, just as it was not instant, emotional, or mystical. When the United States government and the American people became convinced that their security was imperiled unless Great Britain and her allies prevailed, then, and only then, did America join forces with those nations opposing Germany. Spring Rice put it precisely in a letter to Roosevelt in 1915. He asserted that England and France had gone into the war "on high motives (at least it would have been infinite degradation to keep out)." Referring to the United States, he added: "I am not sure that it isn't rather a wise thing to say that a nation will only interfere when its own interests are concerned; otherwise one has an almost endless vista of moral interventions which it is one's patent duty to undertake. . . ."[1] United States entry into the war, in Spring Rice's judgment, was not mandatory on moral grounds but was the result of considerations that had come to define the character of Anglo-American friendship. What if Germany should win, what then for America? America had to support the British and their French allies because

the principles on which our policy is fundamentally based are those to which the U.S.G. "is dedicated"—that proposition of which Lincoln spoke. If in the whole extent of the country there were not one single living man who sympathized with us, we have still with us the dead of Arlington and the words of the dead President who being dead still liveth.

We have nothing to fear from an American America— a German America would be fatal—perhaps an English America equally fatal. For the strength of our race is that wherever we stand, that spot for us is the spot to which we owe our whole allegiance, loyal to our own homes with an entire loyalty, not to a foreign Power whether of our own race or another. It is still the old story of the Puritan —"to walk with God and our fellow-men, according to our own conscience" and not according to the will of king or Emperor or Pope. There is more real community of feeling between men who think the same, according to their own free will and judgment, than between men who act together in obedience to another man, be he who he may. Our kingdom is within us.[2]

With a less poetic thrust, Roosevelt proposed the same argument to Arthur Lee. It was not the German people he feared, but the

Government of Prussianized Germany [which] for the past forty-three years has behaved in such fashion as inevitably to make almost every nation with which it came in contact its foe. . . . It will enter instantly on any career of aggression with cynical brutality and bad faith if it thinks its interests require such action.[3]

[99] Bryce to Roosevelt, June 10, 1911, Bryce Papers.
[100] Roosevelt to Lee, Sept. 25, 1911, Lee Papers.
[101] Roosevelt to Lee, Aug. 14, 1912, *ibid.*
[102] Roosevelt to Spring Rice, Dec. 31, 1912, *Roosevelt Letters* 7: p. 680.
[103] Strachey to Roosevelt, April 8, 1913, Strachey Papers.
[104] Bryce to Roosevelt, Jan. 14, 1913, Fisher, 1929: 2: p. 74.

[1] Spring Rice to Roosevelt, Feb. 23, 1915, Spring Rice Papers.
[2] Spring Rice to Roosevelt, Nov. 26, 1915, *ibid.*
[3] Roosevelt to Lee, Aug. 22, 1914, Lee Papers.

Such complex and subtle judgments were likely to be highly subjective and consequently productive of disagreement, as exemplified by Theodore Roosevelt's running feud with Woodrow Wilson over United States policy toward war in Europe. That Wilson and Roosevelt both privately strongly favored Great Britain in the conflict spoke the reality of spontaneous Anglo-American cordiality within the ruling élite in the United States. But neither man proposed to take the country into the war for any reason other than the protection of vital American interests as each estimated the demands of the situation. They preferred a British victory because English national interest and American national interest naturally identified, a result of almost two decades of diplomatic cooperation and understanding that paralleled a broadening cultural rapport. Theodore Roosevelt became quickly, though not instantly, convinced of the need of American support for the Allies in the defeat of Germany. His attitude toward wartime American policy consequently was colored to a large degree by the failure or refusal of others, especially the American chief of state, to appreciate the issues of the war in the self-same fashion. To his English correspondents he felt free if not compelled to spell out the anger and the frustration which alike assailed him. Out of office and out of power he was impotent in the wake of events. During most of the years crucial to the growth of Anglo-American friendship Roosevelt had occupied the American presidency and in consequence of his power he had acted to promote the national interests and secondarily to further Anglo-American accord. Now in 1914 a war was in progress in Europe which for him threatened to undermine the power of the United States, partly by destroying the world position of America's informal partner in dominion, Great Britain. Such was the peril and Roosevelt, shorn of power and influence, believed he saw the dangers to the nation more clearly than the president or his advisers.

To some of his English circle the problem of England and America after August, 1914, was more complicated than it appeared to Roosevelt, not the least difficulty being that TR was out of office. Whether he was an elder statesman, a potential president, or a used-up politician, it made little immediate difference. Within its own acknowledged definition of national interest, the British government preferred not to offend the United States by its conduct of the war if this could be managed; in effect this meant getting on with Roosevelt's domestic political foes. The focus of its concern had to be on President Wilson and not on ex-President Roosevelt. TR himself recognized this. "Of course I understand that Grey and the British administration must at all costs continue to be on good terms with Wilson and Bryan," he admitted to Arthur Lee early in 1915.[4] As the war lengthened, however,

Roosevelt was less and less able to retain a balanced judgment in the matter. He remarked incisively to Lee in 1918: " . . . I absolutely appreciate the extreme difficulty of the position of the English government. You must stay in with Wilson up to the point where it ceases to be advantageous to England to do so."[5] Bryce had come to grips with the problem in a letter to Roosevelt in 1916, after the two old friends had disagreed over correct United States policy regarding the war. In part he wrote:

It is not for me to tell the U.S. administration their duty though I did distinctly imply my own regret that the President had not protested against the invasion of Belgium. It seems to me that I should have done more harm than good by saying what would have been entirely proper for an American citizen to say (though I do feel just like an American citizen myself.) The friends who have written me from America approving my articles, like Robert Bacon, have not been the pacifists you refer to but vehement anti-Germans and every word I have spoken here and in Parliament and out of it has been to urge a strenuous prosecution of the war without mention of peace till the Germans have been driven from France and Belgium and forced to pay . . . for their detestable wickedness.

Of course we should have been delighted and should be now to have you join us in the war. But could the Administration have got the country to follow? Perhaps you could, had you been President, but it would have been no easy task.[6]

Not one to shirk a difficult task, Theodore Roosevelt showed himself perennially anxious to do exactly what Bryce had spoken of: to lead America into the war.

Awkward relations with some of his major correspondents resulted from the ex-president's resentment over his want of power and influence, since of his longtime friends only St. Loe Strachey and George O. Trevelyan were in no way connected with the British government. Arthur Lee, after active service in France, joined Lloyd George as paraliamentary military secretary at the Ministry of Munitions in October, 1915. James Bryce as a member of the House of Lords authored the famous Bryce Report on German atrocities; but he soon became absorbed in the League of Nations idea, concerning which TR had numerous reservations. Spring Rice found himself in the highly delicate position as H. M. Ambassador to Washington, a post made the more trying because of his old associations with Roosevelt. None of these three men was, therefore, free to support Roosevelt openly in his campaign for American entry into the war, even though they wished for it, lest it cause unfortunate repercussions with the Wilson administration.

As befitted the Anglo-American alliance and the Roosevelt friendships which contributed to it, each of the correspondents felt constrained to espouse those actions which in his individual judgment best served the requirements of his country. The considerable

---

[4] Roosevelt to Lee, Jan. 22, 1915, *ibid.*

[5] Roosevelt to Lee, Feb. 21, 1918, *Roosevelt Letters* **8**: p. 1287.
[6] Bryce to Roosevelt, April 22, 1916, Roosevelt Papers.

strain on certain of the old ties was an inevitable consequence. Roosevelt scored Bryce for his associations with the "world league for peace," asserting that his friend had not made it sufficiently clear that "the prime duty of the great free nations is to prepare themselves against war." [7] St. Loe Strachey seconded TR's displeasure with Bryce.[8] Nor did Spring Rice escape censure. "Of course I am afraid that our dear friend, Springey, whom I love as warmly as you do, has been responsible for a good deal of the appalling mistakes which, in my opinion, our Government has made as regards America," Strachey wrote Roosevelt in 1916. "I have been given to understand that he specially denounced the *Spectator* for its rash and reckless way of talking. . . . I hate writing about Springey, but I expect he has been rather rattled." [9] Such breakdowns of friendship were more apparent than real, stemming from a disagreement over timing or perhaps technique, rather than ultimate purpose. Once the United States came into the war distemper gave way to the old time comradeship. Anticipating American entry into the war Bryce wrote Roosevelt in March, 1917: "I have been trying by letter and pamphlets to make neutrals . . . in your western States realize the supreme moral issues [of the war]. Needless to say how grateful we all are to you for your incessant activity in that direction. May success crown them!" [10] "I am doing all I can right along the lines you mentioned," Roosevelt replied cordially.[11] Disagreement over timing and technique would, nevertheless, test the durability of the Anglo-American entente. While Woodrow Wilson watched events, deliberated over their meaning for the United States, and searched for methods other than arms, to uphold national honor and interest, Theodore Roosevelt had come rapidly to the conclusion as to what America must do: go to war. This he told his English friends time and again in countless ways. Without doubt they all valued his support and though those officially representing H. M. Government, like Spring Rice, feared that the colonel's zeal might do harm as well as good, in the privacy of their minds they believed that American entrance into the war would be a fulfillment of their growing friendship, "the consummation, at long last, of a very special relationship." [12]

Though Theodore Roosevelt's reactions to World War I were at first unsettled and it was some three months before he spoke out publicly and unequivocally for the defeat of Germany and support for Great Britain and her allies by positive American action,

from the onset his private sympathies for England were unambiguous. "I can not forbear writing you just a word of affectionate sympathy in the very hard time you are having in England," he noted to Arthur Lee in late August, 1914. "Thank Heaven! at least you do not have to suffer what the continental nations are suffering." And he continued: "I thought England behaved exactly as she ought to behave, and with very great dignity. It was a fine thing." [13] Two weeks later he reiterated these sentiments, again in a letter to Lee. "I can not refrain from sending you a line of affection and sympathy in these terrible and trying hours . . . the British army has fought admirably. . . . The attitude of the English people seems to be on the whole admirable." And later on in the same letter:

With all your suffering you are playing a heroic part, and whatever Germany's success or failure on the continent, England is certain to win now as she was to win against Napoleon a century ago if only she will be true to herself; and so far she has given every proof that she intends to be true to herself.

He then proceeded to describe Edward Grey as a "statesman of the Timoleon and John Hampden, the Washington and the Lincoln school," neither "a party to wrong-doing" nor afraid "to draw the sword rather than submit to wrong doing." [14] Such feelings were warmly received and returned by Roosevelt's English friends.[15] Sir George O. Trevelyan wrote in September, 1914, a particularly effusive letter, part of which read:

. . . it is of untold importance that you should have a leading part at this conjuncture of events. . . . The need of you is not for the present only, inasmuch as a vast number of intricate problems will arise during the war, and after the war, on the bold and just solution of which the welfare of countless millions must depend . . . perhaps you are, of all other living men, the one who is most bound to serve the world, let alone his people by his guidance.

In saying all this Trevelyan found his justification in Roosevelt's "mode of thought on international policy" and his "deep and wide interest in the history of the past"—both of which had been crucial elements in the build-up of the Anglo-American rapprochement from 1898.[16]

Along with his expression of personal concern went some clear indication of what TR's public attitude on the war was to be, and consequently the policy of involvement which he came to espouse.

. . . It seems to me that if I were President I should register a very emphatic protest, a protest that would mean something, against the levy of the huge war contribution on Belgium. As regards Belgium, there is not even room for argument. The Germans, to suit their own purposes, trampled on their solemn obligations to Belgium and on Belgium's rights,

[7] Roosevelt to Bryce, March 31, 1915, Bryce Papers. Roosevelt was critical of Bryce in letters to Lee, Jan. 22, 1915 and March 6, 1915, Lee Papers.

[8] Strachey to Roosevelt, April 27, 1915, Strachey Papers.

[9] Strachey to Roosevelt, Sept. 23, 1916, *ibid.*

[10] Bryce to Roosevelt, March 21, 1917, Bryce Papers.

[11] Roosevelt to Bryce, April 19, 1917, *ibid.* See also Spring Rice to Roosevelt, April 19, 1917, Gwynn, 1929: 2: p. 396; Roosevelt to Spring Rice, June 19, 1917, *ibid.*, pp. 396–397.

[12] Allen, 1955; p. 690.

[13] Roosevelt to Lee, Aug. 22, 1914, Lee Papers.

[14] Roosevelt to Lee, Sept. 4, 1914, *ibid.*

[15] For example, Lee to Roosevelt, Aug. 15, 1914, *ibid;* Spring Rice to Roosevelt, Sept. 10, 1914, Gwynn, 1929: 2: pp. 227–228.

[16] Trevelyan to Roosevelt, Sept. 1, 1914, Roosevelt Papers.

he told Lee.[17] In this connection he remarked to Spring Rice: "Of course I would not have made such a statement unless I was willing to back it up." [18] The violation of Belgian neutrality was one of the arguments TR advanced most strenuously for opposing Germany. His letters early in the war also underscored his contempt for the "peace at any price" men. "They have passed a procession of idiotic universal arbitration treaties with Paraguay and other similar world powers," he noted to Lee, and "all the apostles of the utterly inane scream joyfully that this shows that the United States does not need any battleships, and that if Europe had only had these treaties there would never have been any war!" [19] To Roosevelt, after the events of 1914, peace advocates were nothing but "prize jacks," a new strain of the American copperhead.

In the fall of 1914 some talk of peace could be heard —the Western Front had not yet become the stalemate of attrition. Roosevelt and Spring Rice explored the outlook. "None of the Powers so far has shown any anxiety to offer peace terms or accept mediation," Spring Rice pointed out in September, "but it is quite certain that the Secretary of State [Bryan] will do his best to bring about peace, and that the other side will do their best to prove they wanted peace but that we declined it." Afraid of being outmaneuvered, Spring Rice thought it not impossible that Bryan, whom he referred to as "the Father of Words," would be hoodwinked by the Germans. He wrote TR that Edward Grey "longs for peace, but it must be a peace that gives satisfaction to Belgium for all she has suffered, and a sure guarantee of the future." [20] Spring Rice accused the Germans of talking peace only to make the Allies appear as the "bloody-minded ruffians who brought on the war for the destruction of Germany—and Germany the innocent sufferer." [21] Apart from his contempt for what he considered German perfidy, Roosevelt appreciated the obstacles in the way of peace-making. In a letter dated October 3, 1914, he admitted to Spring Rice that in 1905 he had acted in the Russo-Japanese war only after he had "received explicit assurances . . . that my action would be welcome." [22] As weeks became months, peace became more and more remote and the Western Front a gruesome reality. The colonel dismissed the peace advocates with growing abruptness; they were a reminder of certain people in the North during the American Civil War who shouted for peace —"these to a man voted against Abraham Lincoln," he told Spring Rice. And he observed further: ". . . if

in that year [1864] England and France had joined as certain of their politicians wished them to join, in offering mediation so as to bring about 'peace,' we should have treated it as an unfriendly act." [23] No less than his English friends, Roosevelt was sure the war would have to be fought through to a conclusive victory, not for the sake of civilization—for he doubted the moral soundness of the Russians and suspected the pretensions of the Japanese—but for the sake of the Anglo-American way and their dominion in the world.[24]

The initial assessments of Roosevelt and his English friends toward the war—England doing its duty, America in need of a great leader, proponents of peace suspected as German tools or dupes—all these drew upon the reservoir of goodwill and understanding that had more and more typified Anglo-American relations in the first years of the twentieth century. Serious divergencies arose when Great Britain countered the intensive German submarine effort by a campaign of search and seizure of neutral vessels, including those of American registry. Such British actions caused a crisis in Anglo-American friendship as seen in the letters of Roosevelt and his correspondents, in addition to the official crisis between London and Washington. The resolution of these difficulties, as proposed by Roosevelt and his friends in their desire for United States military participation, anticipated the very solution eventually adopted by the Wilson administration, and one that pointed the way to continued Anglo-American accord.

In a syndicated newspaper article of November 22, 1914, "The Peace-maker, The Navy," Roosevelt sharply criticized both the German U-boat campaign and British counter-moves. Respecting the English actions, he contended that England had violated American neutrality while exercising considerable ingenuity in making herself appear as the injured party.[25] In light of this charge, it is instructive to read Spring Rice's letter to his old friend, dated November 5, 1914. After observing that "neutrality questions are very complicated," Spring Rice took the attitude that his country was only "enforcing the doctrine of continuous voyage which the American Supreme Court always maintained in the case of importations from Nassau during the Civil War." Then he added significantly: "But the feeling is growing that the American flag ought *not* to be stopped on the high seas or American ships examined." As a good Englishman and conscientious ambassador he, nonetheless, restated the familar justification for the controversial actions of the Royal Navy with conviction, while disavowing that these were of necessity his own views in the matter.

But we are fighting for our life and must defend ourselves —that really we are fighting for American principles of

[17] Roosevelt to Lee, Aug. 22, 1914, Lee Papers.
[18] Roosevelt to Spring Rice, Oct. 3, 1914, *Roosevelt Letters* 8: p. 821.
[19] Roosevelt to Lee, Sept. 4, 1914, Lee Papers.
[20] Spring Rice to Roosevelt, Sept. 10, 1914, Gwynn, 1929: 2: p. 229.
[21] Spring Rice to Roosevelt, Sept. 16, 1914, Spring Rice Papers.
[22] Roosevelt to Spring Rice, Oct. 13, 1914, *Roosevelt Letters* 8: p. 822.

[23] *Ibid.*
[24] *Ibid.*
[25] Roosevelt, *Works* 20: pp. 122–135; p. 123.

liberty and that if we are downed the U.S. will suffer: that the U.S. ought therefore to allow a little latitude and not enforce its uttermost rights in favor of oil and copper when this is to our detriment.   That the U.S. never raised a whisper about the Hague Convention but as soon as we enforce the American doctrine of continuous voyage . . . there is a general howl.[26]

The answer Roosevelt made to these remarks, which included the inevitable phrase "if I were president," was not so much anti-British as it was pro-American in its tone, and not a little self-righteous.

I would not allow the British or any other people to exercise the right of search; but this would be because I would as emphatically interfere on behalf of neutral Belgium and would no less emphatically have prevented our people from doing anything in the way of violation of neutrality, so I would feel entirely at liberty to exact the justice I was giving.

At the close of this particular letter, which contained a long and repetitious argument of wartime rights and wrongs, Roosevelt, perceiving the acute distress of his old friend, wrote: "You must be under a great strain, old man, and I am very sorry for you." [27]   Though the issue between the two nations, as between the friends, was real, one and all they approached it as a difficulty to be settled and not a controversy that should be allowed to mushroom into a diplomatic rupture.

Early in 1915 Roosevelt spoke his mind on Anglo-American maritime problems to Arthur Lee.   His position he crisply stated in an enclosure accompanying a short letter.   The pertinent passage was as follows.

In international matters we should treat each nation on its conduct and without the slightest reference to the fact that a larger or smaller proportion of its blood flows in the veins of our own citizens.   I have publicly and emphatically taken the ground for Belgium and I wish that the United States would take ground for Belgium, because I hold that this is our duty, and that Germany's conduct toward Belgium demands that we antagonize her in this matter as far as Belgium is concerned, and that we emphatically and in practical shape try to see that Belgium's wrongs are redressed.   Because of the British attitude toward Belgium I have publicly and emphatically approved of this attitude and of Great Britain's conduct in living up to her obligations by defending Belgium, even at the cost of war.   But I am not doing this on any ground that there is any "hands across the sea" alliance, explicit or implicit, with England. I have never used in peace or war any such expression as "hands across the sea" and I emphatically disapprove of what it signifies save in so far as it means cordial friendship between us and any other nation that acts in accordance with the standards that we deem just and right.[28]

To Lee, on the other hand, the problems dividing the two countries were symptomatic of a deeper dilemma: the uncertain response of any man who is asked to sacrifice vital interests for the sake of friendship.   "It has been a great delight to be at home for even such a short time," Lee wrote Roosevelt while back from the Front,

but whilst I have been here, I have necessarily heard a great deal which is very disquieting about the alleged waning of public sympathy in America for the cause of the Allies.   I do not mean, of course, amongst the educated or responsible people, but amongst the masses who naturally have little, if anything to go on, except what they read in the newspapers or what they see at the Cinema Shows.

This loss of support, Lee thought, was due not alone to the American government's attitude toward contraband, but to the failure of good press relations.   ". . . The only real war news, written by Americans who are known and trusted by the American public, comes from the German side, whilst even sympathisers with the cause of the Allies can hear nothing whatever about the trials and tribulations of the British and the French armies."   He blamed the London government for not giving American reporters greater accessibility to the Front and urged Roosevelt to press Lord Grey about the need for improved American coverage of the war from the Anglo-French side.   As for the colonel's own public utterances on the war, Lee was enthusiastic, though mindfully private in his mention of it.   "I saw enough of your articles to make me very grateful," he informed TR, and "to make me want to work a willing horse still further."   Nor was an altogether personal concern lacking in this wartime letter.   "I was sorry not to see Ethel and Dick [29] again before they left France. They really did a splendid job there, and if only our Army had not moved away from their area of operations, I should have been able to see them often." [30] Nevertheless, the problem of neutral rights had not been dispelled.   TR put it bluntly to St. Loe Strachey at this time: "There has been an unpleasant resemblance in this war to what was done over a century ago when the Berlin and Milan decrees of Napoleon and the British Orders in Council rendered it hopeless for a neutral to expect good treatment from either belligerent." [31]

The exchange of thoughts between St. Loe Strachey and Roosevelt in February, 1915, of which the foregoing comment was a part, was also significant because it contained in the words of each friend an almost identical statement of the nature of the Anglo-American special relationship, even as it was under great stress.   The tendency of some of Roosevelt's correspondents to obscure the line of distinction between England and America by reason of appeal to some higher moral or racial norm—and Strachey himself could be guilty of this on occasion—made it particularly useful to under-

---

[26] Spring Rice to Roosevelt, Nov. 5, 1914, Roosevelt Papers.
[27] Roosevelt to Spring Rice, Nov. 11, 1914, *Roosevelt Letters* 8: pp. 840–841.
[28] Roosevelt to Lee, Jan. 2, 1915, Lee Papers.

[29] Roosevelt's daughter, Ethel, and her husband, Richard Derby, a medical doctor who were in France with the American Ambulance Service.
[30] Lee to Roosevelt, Jan. 8, 1915, Lee Papers.
[31] Roosevelt to Strachey, Feb. 22, 1915, *Roosevelt Letters* 8: p. 899; see also to Spring Rice, Feb. 5, 1915, *ibid.*, p. 888.

score the distinction.[32]   At this time Strachey wrote: "Though I love America and have always loved her ever since I was a boy, I do not of course in the least profess to put America in my affections on the same level with my own country, or anywhere near it.   I should be a miserable creature if I did." [33]   In his reply Roosevelt spoke directly to this conviction:

You exactly meet my view when you say that while you love America you do not in the least place America on the same level in your affections as your own country or anywhere near it.   This is exactly the attitude you ought to take.   It is exactly the attitude I take about America and England; and I am convinced that it makes it far more possible for Englishmen and Americans to be cordial and deep friends when they take this attitude than when they slop and indulge in insincere gush, which makes both sides look like hypocrites when their actions are compared with their words.[34]

Theodore Roosevelt believed that sentiment was a luxury neither country could afford because it might entail the sacrifice of their national interests.

For a confidant like Strachey it was an easier matter to appreciate the realities and limitations of Anglo-American accord than for the English public at large. Theodore Roosevelt's image in England in 1915, derived especially from his magazine articles dealing with the war (some of which had appeared separately) in addition to a 1915 collection of his wartime essays, did not exhibit a clear and vigorous stand for the Allied cause.   The average Englishman thought he had reason to expect a total support of Britain which TR was unable to offer.   The ex-president had found it necessary to denounce both the German violation of Belgium along with the submarine war and British disregard for neutral rights on the high seas.   His arguments justifying these views were read by the English man in the street.   At the same time the average Englishman was aware of Roosevelt's excoriation of the Wilson administration's failure to act in behalf of Belgium even by verbal protest or to act effectively in the name of American maritime rights.   As Strachey told Roosevelt:

I expect most Englishmen in their present state of tension —and please do not think that I am free of such tension and excitement, because of course I am not—will be a little sore at what they will think your coolness towards England and your desire to be as sympathetic so far as you can to Germany.   I won't deny that the natural man in me makes me wish that you could have been a little warmer.   At

the same time my head if not my heart tells me that it is a very great advantage that you should have been so cool to us, as it makes your condemnation of the United States action as regards Belgium so much more telling.   No one can say that you are taking the line you do merely out of friendliness to us.

At the same time Strachey urged Roosevelt to understand the circumstances in England.   "We have seemed very calm, but the temper here exactly corresponds with the temper of your people of the North during the Civil War.   We will brook no interference with what we deem our right to resist a ruthless and remorseless enemy." [35]   In return Roosevelt was able to explain to Strachey, as distinguished from the public at large, more precisely and more in a spirit of evident friendship why he had written as he had.

You say that most Englishmen are a little sore at what they consider my coolness towards England . . . and my desire to be just to Germany.   I expect this.   At the same time remember that I emphatically stated that England was right; and that England had made all lovers of peace her debtors by her action toward Belgium; but I thought it very unwise to indulge in hysterics in the matter.   I am trying to look at things dispassionately. . . . Next to my own country I put England first; I am in closest sympathy with her.

Given the nature of the friendship, this meant that Roosevelt thought the United States should not take a certain view of things merely because that represented Great Britain's position also.   Thus he wrote to Strachey: "while I most deeply sympathize with your feelings and realize the great tension you are under, yet I cannot accept your view from your own standpoint as regards your attitude toward neutral vessels." [36] In so far as neutral rights were involved in early 1915, Roosevelt and his English friends were separated by their respective national requirements.

The United States did not submit to the logic of the British stand on neutral rights.   The actions of the Germans, on the other hand, made it possible for Roosevelt and for other Americans as well, to identify themselves with England on grounds of moral rectitude. The German march across Belgium in defiance of treaty obligations and the German submarine war in defiance of humanity were sufficient cause for Roosevelt to abandon neutrality.   "Personally I have come more and more to the conviction that neutrality when a great moral issue is at stake is all wrong, because it amounts to neutrality between right and wrong; and that is the equivalent to taking a stand against right," the colonel asserted to Arthur Lee early in 1915.[37]   Yet it is instructive to explore the distinction TR offered between abstract injustice as a reason for going to war—or as a consideration of the Anglo-American view of what was morally wrong and thus must be opposed—and the

---

[32] For example, Strachey to Roosevelt, March 19, 1915; to Roosevelt, Oct. 26, 1915, Strachey Papers.   "Between ourselves your plain speaking was most useful to me for I had tried to say the same thing but I was smiled at, on the grounds that I could know nothing about America or Americans as I had only been three weeks in America and therefore superior people at the Foreign Office must know better." Strachey to Roosevelt, Dec. 15, 1916, *ibid.*   See also Trevelyan to Roosevelt, Jan. 8, 1915, Roosevelt Papers.

[33] Strachey to Roosevelt, Feb. 1, 1915, Roosevelt Papers.

[34] Roosevelt to Strachey, Feb. 22, 1915, *Roosevelt Letters* 8: p. 897.

[35] Strachey to Roosevelt, Feb. 1, 1915, Roosevelt Papers.

[36] Roosevelt to Strachey, Feb. 22, 1915, *Roosevelt Letters* 8: p. 897.

[37] Roosevelt to Lee, Feb. 26, 1915, Lee Papers.

manner in which Roosevelt thought of the pressing moral issue of the war." "The neutrality of our Government now boasts," he reminded Strachey, "like yours in '61 . . . serves ease and selfishness at the moment; but it does not serve morality nor in the long run, not national interest." [38] In other words, national interest suffered from an immoral policy, a factor which for both Roosevelt and his English friends had been a touchstone of policy. Despite Britain's failure to protest the German invasion of Belgium under the Hague Convention, the British nonetheless had gone to war against Germany, a nation that had acted immorally. Roosevelt consequently called upon his fellow Americans to enter the war and support the Allies. "It is better to argue the case on Belgium being wrong than Britain being right"—such were the practicalities of the situation he told Lee. [39] Strachey came close to describing the issue perfectly in a letter to TR of March, 1915:

I felt it would be a very mean thing for me or any other Englishman to try to claim you as pro-British because you were taking the splendid line that you took as to the moral obligations imposed on your country. I did not, that is, want your enemies to say that the *Spectator* had docketed you as pro-British when your were only intensely pro-American. [40]

Yet in another perspective, was not the morality herein referred to an instance of being true to what Roosevelt and his friends conceived of as the common Anglo-American commitment to righteousness? Both George O. Trevelyan and St. Loe Strachey thought it so, as letters they sent along to Roosevelt showed. The former wrote early in 1915.

You are giving such notable testimony to your friendship for England, and for the cause which is so much greater and more far-reaching even than England. The protest against destruction of the industrial and pacific communities of Europe, and against the revivals of barbaric warfare, is worthy of the most awful risks on the part of such a race as ours. [41]

For Strachey the "blood ties" of England with American held the same lesson.

I dare say I am wrong in making so much of the blood ties between America and England but after all I have a good deal of excuse. My direct ancestor, William Strachey, was the first secretary of the Colony of Virginia, and so, as one American historian told me once, I may consider myself "founders' kin" of the United States. . . . Besides when I see the way the English language eats up all other tongues that have come to America and still more how the English common law and the standards of English justice, of right and wrong, universally prevail, can we help but remember your English, Scottish and Irish origin? [42]

Out of habit acquired from history and experience Roosevelt and his friends viewed the world dominance of the Anglo-Americans as morally fitting, so that their reaction to the war, which was a challenge to them and their power, displayed this accountably moral strain.

Once Theodore Roosevelt had come to the decision that neutrality for the United States was an untenable moral position, and a national disgrace, he became wary of anyone who, irrespective of circumstance or motivation, appeared less emphatic than he about America's part in the war. His views, which he continued to publish in the United States in *Metropolitan* and which were frequently reprinted in Great Britain brought him into open disagreement with some of his old friends. Spring Rice, for example, thought it proper to caution TR in his strictures on the Wilson administration. Though Spring Rice applauded such criticisms in favor of Belgium and against America's inaction, restraint was nonetheless appropriate in his opinion. "A quarrel [between England and America] at this moment would be disastrous," he told Roosevelt in February, 1915. [43] Of his long-term correspondents Roosevelt had perhaps the gravest misgivings about James Bryce, as was brought out in a long letter he wrote to him, dated March 31, 1915. Bryce, active in promoting a postwar association or league of nations, had written approvingly of United States neutrality in the war. To TR neutrality had become an indefensible position, while talk of postwar associations was inopportune until the Germans had been soundly beaten. The colonel accused the ex-ambassador of "playing Wilson's game," i.e., neutrality for the United States, and compared his attitude to that of a supporter of Lincoln in the Civil War who endorsed the Gladstone-Palmerston policy as well. He urged Bryce to be more in the style of Henry Ward Beecher who preached the Union cause in England and who was not interested in peace movements, just as in 1915 the United States ought not to be concerned with talk of peace. Laboring this theme, Roosevelt observed that if Wilson's policy was right, "then it is foolishness for an American to protest the unrighteousness of German conquest of Belgium or the righteousness of the English position." Perhaps the last paragraph of this letter contained one of the most salient statements of the Anglo-American entente as TR conceived it.

In the past, most of our pacifists have gushed and shrieked about "Anglo-Saxon brother" and "hands across the sea" and "peace, peace, peace"; I have never gone into any of these manifestations; but when the time of stress came these gentry have shudderingly clamored against taking any effective stand for England when England was fighting for the right; whereas I, who have never gushed about

[38] Roosevelt to Strachey, Feb. 22, 1915, *Roosevelt Letters* 8: p. 933.

[39] Roosevelt to Lee, March 16, 1915, Lee Papers.

[40] Strachey to Roosevelt, March 15, 1915, Strachey Papers.

[41] Trevelyan to Roosevelt, Jan. 8, 1915, Roosevelt Papers.

[42] Strachey to Roosevelt, March 19, 1915, Strachey Papers.

[43] Spring Rice to Roosevelt, Feb. 5, 1915, Roosevelt Papers; see also Spring Rice to Roosevelt, Nov. 22, 1915, Spring Rice Papers.

arbitration in the past, have stood for concrete right in the present.[44]

How profoundly Bryce's behavior disturbed Roosevelt can be gauged by a letter he sent to Strachey, also written in March, 1915. The ex-president commented at length.

Mr. Bryce has furnished the strongest argument that can be furnished to justify the action of Americans including Wilson and Bryan who have leaned against the Allies and in favor of Germany during the war. . . . It is utterly futile to be favorable to the Allies and yet uphold the Administration.
I have counselled as strongly as I know how that the British Government should exercise not as a matter of good will to the American people but because of its own interest, the utmost self-command in dealing with America and yield to the protests of the administration wherever it possibly can; I have counselled this in the interests of England and along exactly the lines of the argument employed by John Bright in his letters to Sumner during the Civil War; when John Bright utterly opposed the conduct of Palmerston and Gladstone toward the United States but wished the United States Government to be sure not to give justification to the war party in England. At that time Henry Ward Beecher went to England, where he had some reputation, so as to state the Union and the anti-Slavery causes. I had hoped that Bryce, because of his great reputation here, would use that reputation in stating the English cause and even more the Belgian cause to the American people. But he has not!
Apparently he [Bryce] and a number of other people in England are always anxious to justify the enemies of England precisely as so many people in America as regards actions like that whereby I took Panama and the like, are always anxious to justify the enemies of the United States. It is the existence of the types of Maxsie in England and Pulitzer in the United States which make it wise for men like yourself and myself not to gush or become over-effusive about the relations between the two countries; but sanely to work for friendship between them, and *above all when strain comes always to make our words exactly back up our feelings.* I have never gushed over England. . . .[45]

Strachey was of much the same mind as his American friend.

I abound in all you say about Bryce's ridiculous encouragement of the Washington Government. It must have been terribly exasperating to men like you who were determined as possible to make your country speak out and not commit the criminal folly of trying to be neutral on a moral issue. Bryce of course gave the time-serving and timid just the

excuse they wanted, the excuse of being able to say that you and your supporters were more British than the British Government.[46]

Trevelyan also sent a note of encouragement at this time.

This morning I read the sentence in which you set forth the *moral* side of the munitions question—whether they were to be employed for the rescue of Belgium, or her continued enslavement. The reading of it kindled into flame the smoldering consciousness that there is a man in the world who is never wanting of high national duty. You know that you are my hero and always will be; and there is no need to enlarge on that topic.[47]

Just a week before Trevelyan penned these lines of characteristic praise, the Cunard liner *Lusitania* was torpedoed and sunk by a German submarine off the south coast of Ireland. The moral issues of the war gained new urgency.

The *Lusitania* disaster dramatized German perfidy but it also found Roosevelt admiring German efficiency as contrasted with the relative inefficiency of the English-speaking nations. "We of the English-speaking peoples have acted precisely in the spirit set forth and condemned in Kipling's famous poem about the 'flannelled fool at the wicket, the muddied oaf in the goals,'" he exclaimed to Arthur Lee. As for America: "Most emphatically, if we had done what we ought to have done after the sinking of the *Lusitania,* I and my four boys would now be in the army getting ready to serve with you in Flanders or else to serve against Constantinople." Referring to Bryan's resignation as secretary of state in the aftermath of the loss of the *Lusitania,* TR told Lee that he thought Wilson's policy of strict accountability meant little change in actual fact. "He and Bryan apparently agree with cordiality that our policy should be one of milk and water. They only disagree as to the precise quantity of dilution in the mixture."[48] In his insistence upon the need to oppose the immorality of German behavior—the sinking of the *Lusitania* now offered as a final piece of evidence—he continued to get encouragement from several of his English correspondents. Trevelyan was especially fervent in his appeals. "If only America would speak out! The stand-off attitude of the Washington government is having a subtle and fatal effect on the future of mankind," he contended.

The fixed resolution of the most powerful of democratic nations to refuse any recognition of international issues of public law and morality had had a profound effect on smaller nations . . . all the circle of smaller neutrals have felt justified in blinding themselves to questions of right and wrong and guided their course entirely by considerations of self-interest. . . . One clear and outspoken declaration from America that they will not see Belgium and

[44] Roosevelt to Bryce, March 31, 1915, *Roosevelt Letters* **8**: pp. 897, 918. Bryce and Roosevelt continued to exchange views on war and peace down to the entry of the United States into the conflict. Bryce's tone was invariably one of measured friendship; see, for example, Bryce to Roosevelt, April 22, 1916, Roosevelt Papers, wherein he wrote approvingly of TR's candor: "I am glad you have expressed yourself freely and openly as a friend might." Roosevelt's attitude was more like anger; for example, Roosevelt to Bryce, June 19, 1918, *Roosevelt Letters* **8**: p. 1067. "Wilson is the most lamentable example we have ever seen of the success of that kind of demogogue who appeals to the educated incompetents of the *Evening Post* and *Atlantic Monthly* type, the President Eliot type."
[45] Roosevelt to Strachey, March 23, 1915, Strachey Papers. (Italics in original.)
[46] Strachey to Roosevelt, April 27, 1915, *ibid.* (Italics in original.)
[47] Trevelyan to Roosevelt, May 13, 1915, Roosevelt Papers.
[48] Roosevelt to Lee, June 17, 1915, *Roosevelt Letters* **8**: pp. 935–940 *passim.*

Armenia and Serbia ground to powder would set this great controversy in its true light and would be worth to humanity and public right a thousand battalions and fifty Dreadnoughts.[49]

Such was the disillusionment of some Englishmen arising from the failure of the Wilson administration to act in their behalf in the name of righteousness.

Roosevelt, too, continued to pour out his frustrations over United States policy to his English friends, a frustration making him less and less tolerant not only of the Wilson government but of those groups he believed Wilson curried favor with. In August, 1915, he told Lee he was preparing an article for *Metropolitan* "attacking the pacifists and the German-American proposals and the proposals of the beef barons and the cotton barons to prevent the exportation of arms and munitions to the Allies." He deemed the pacifists the "most ignoble set I have ever known. It seems incredible that they should be willing to play the game of the German aggressors by cutting off supplies from those endeavoring to right the wrongs of Belgium."[50] The article referred to was the famous assault on "hyphenated Americans," which appeared in the October, 1915 issue of *Metropolitan*. It was a massive indictment of the German-Americans especially, whom TR accused of being "Germans in America."[51] The article also contained a vigorous statement of what Roosevelt had been saying consistently to his English friends: "Most emphatically I myself am not an Englishman, once removed! I am straight United States!"[52] After reading the article Strachey wrote: "Many thanks for sending me the *Metropolitan* article on 'hyphenated Americanism.' I always love to read anything by you."[53] What Roosevelt had asserted in the article, with regard to the bonds of race between the Anglo-Americans, had been a working principle of the alliance as he and his friends had conceived of it for a long time.

The more certain Theodore Roosevelt became about the duty of the United States to enter the war, the more concerned he was by the lack of American military preparedness. "There is a chance that the Germans will kick even Wilson into the war," he exclaimed to Lee on one occasion; "but he won't go into the war unless he is kicked; and he will go in utterly unprepared."[54] In the August, 1915, *Metropolitan* the former chief executive had written an article, "Peace Insurance by Preparedness Against War," in which he concluded: "The most certain way for a nation to invite disaster is to be opulent, self-assertive, and unarmed. Preparedness against war is the only efficient form of national peace insurance."[55] At this very time England was undergoing a great debate over the propriety of compulsory military service, with Arthur Lee publicly enjoining the British government to adopt a general draft for the Forces. Roosevelt congratulated him on his efforts, saying: "as you know, I have now for a year been urging this country to adopt universal service and in the next article I write I shall quote what you have said,"[56] a promise he kept in "Uncle Sam's Only Friend is Uncle Sam," appearing in *Metropolitan*, November, 1915.[57] St. Loe Strachey, who years before had expressed fear that America was too "drowned in security" to recognize the necessity of military preparedness sent the former president an enthusiastic letter of support.

Last Monday walking on the shores near here [Strachey was writing from Wales] I planned a letter to you as to the great, nay, *terrible uneasiness* I feel about America's "unguarded situation"—to use an old phrase. I felt that now things were going better with us as I believe they are, that I could express my fears about America without seeming to be trying to drag America into the present war. I know of course that you would never take such a line, still while we were in a tight place the feeling for silence was imperative. Rightly or wrongly however I believe we are now out of danger. . . . It pains me like a blow in the face to think that even temporarily the American people should be sunk into a morass of rhetorical cant and slushy sentiment. It is most incomprehensible. If you had all turned real Quakers I could understand and in a sense sympathize. But you have not. I feel that any moment the American people might still make a mad rush into the war without preparation or any counting of the cost. For example, Japan. I should still not be surprized to hear of the state of California putting some intolerable insult upon the Japanese.

You take a very wise and practical line in your article. I should like to see a standing army of 250,000. It would among other things give a form of service to your idle rich young men and strain a number of men who, after say ten years in the service, could be used for all sorts of public service. . . . If not, I suppose you will have to go through the fiery ordeal either of a war in which you will be temporarily beaten by some South American state or else be hit hard on the head by Japan. This of course is all on the assumption that we win the war and win *absolutely*. . . . When the war is over and the Allies have demobilized, the Germans will present to you a bill of, say £ 300,000,000, based on the Alabama (I never could spell) analogy, and you will be told to pay up at once. You will of course refuse and then you will find that all Wilson's toleration of Germany instead of making you friends of Berlin only inspired the feeling that you were good stuff to bully.[58]

A short while later Strachey reiterated his views. "It exasperates me as a friend of America to think that your country should be gambling on our success, for that is what it comes to. I do not in the least believe

---

[49] Trevelyan to Roosevelt, Nov. 7, 1915, Roosevelt Papers.
[50] Roosevelt to Lee, Aug. 6, 1915, *Roosevelt Letters* 8: p. 960; see also Roosevelt to Lee, Sept. 2, 1915, *ibid.*, pp. 966–971.
[51] Roosevelt, "International Duty and Hyphenated Americans," *Works* 20: pp. 324–343.
[52] *Ibid.*, p. 329.
[53] Strachey to Roosevelt, Oct. 26, 1915, Strachey Papers.
[54] Roosevelt to Lee, Aug. 6, 1915, *Roosevelt Letters* 8: p. 960.

[55] Roosevelt, *Works*, 20: pp. 344–373; 372–373.
[56] Roosevelt to Lee, Sept. 2, 1915, *Roosevelt Letters* 8: p. 966.
[57] Roosevelt, *Works* 20: pp. 374–392; 385.
[58] Strachey to Roosevelt, Sept. 15, 1915, Strachey Papers. (Italics in original.)

that Wilson is capable of putting the country into a proper posture of defense, so I suppose things will drift on any how." [59]   Only James Bryce entered a dissenting opinion on the subject of universal military service, sounding chords from the Anglo-American historical commitment that, to some at least, had a peculiar discordance in 1915. "One of the deepest English traditions is against compulsion in any form," he reminded TR. "It is a sentiment, almost a religion, among the masses. Every sensible man recognizes that it [conscription] may be necessary but also wishes to avoid it if possible, because much resistance would have to be overcome. It is not fear that prompts resistance but a dislike of being compelled." [60]   Such convictions so boldy stated only deepened the estrangement that existed between Roosevelt and Bryce.

In these months of late 1915 the ex-president, *hors de combat,* found solace largely in his pen. At the last of that year he and Spring Rice were in frequent communication by letter. The war had not effaced the Britisher's sardonic streak. Commenting on Roosevelt's magazine articles that dealt with the war, he wrote:

You have done your best to bring your own country as well as ours to what you thought was its duty. Also that no American statesman can be expected to refrain from the national habit of speaking ill of our country, however great the crisis. No doubt under similar circumstances British statesmen would do the same, or (what is more correct to say) *have* done the same.

So curious a mixture of sentiment and *realpolitik,* while perhaps characteristic of Spring Rice, should not be allowed to obscure the deeper feelings of regard he retained for Roosevelt and for America; he closed his letter assuring his friend that the British Government "have a right regard for you whatever you may have of them." [61]   Apart from personal disagreements, there were matters of state as well which the ambassador chose to discuss with the ex-president. For example, a word from Roosevelt at the right time could be useful in shoring up the Anglo-French alliance. Spring Rice appraised it this way. Some of what TR had written for publication, according to Spring Rice, was being quoted by certain people to give the impression that England was neglecting her duty toward France. Further, he informed Roosevelt,

German agents have been using material provided in great quantities by Englishmen who are (no doubt for good reasons) criticizing their own government as heavily as Lincoln's government was attacked. . . . Unfortunately the agents of which I spoke have used your great name and prestige abroad for the purpose of conveying the impression that England was neglecting her duties incumbent upon her as an ally of France. This has done the Allied

cause a great deal of harm as you see many Englishmen complain of what you have done. . . . [62]

Roosevelt's response to all this followed two lines. He openly disagreed with the provocative comment that "no American statesman (meaning myself) can be expected to refrain from the national pastime of 'speaking ill' of England. I had supposed that you had read my article," he remonstrated, "and can only ask that you now read it. In that article I certainly speak far more ill of the United States and of Germany than of England. . . . I say nothing of praise of America whatever. I speak in the heartiest praise of the British Navy and of her army at the front. I particularly explain that England has done better than we would have done." [63]   On the level of policy, TR offered to write a letter "to a Frenchman, say Hanotaux, that the Allies shall stand together to the end." [64]   Though he drafted such a letter it was never sent, largely on the advice of the French ambassador, Jusserand. That the passing disagreement between Roosevelt and Spring Rice was dispelled was clear from a letter of Spring Rice, dated November 25, 1915. He apologized for his earlier letters, as "written off in haste and I seem to have joked with difficulty." [65]   A few days later another letter from Spring Rice to Roosevelt lamented the anti-war propaganda in America and in Europe; it was more persuasive than many supposed. Vallandingham, he wrote "was a good type of the sort of man we shall have to deal with in Europe for the next six months or so." The ambassador recommended Lincoln's cure. "We can send friends of peace over to the enemy for his edification." [66]   On a personal and a policy level Spring Rice entertained few doubts about the desirability of an Anglo-American comradeship in arms.

As Britain and her allies faced the winter of 1915–1916 Spring Rice's pessimism, which heavily colored his ambassadorial dispatches to the Foreign Office, was not unwarranted. Roosevelt got a full and frank account of things in England in a long letter from Arthur Lee, dated January 26, 1916. By that time Lee had settled in at his job at the Munitions Ministry, where "my principal duty is to act as Lloyd George's deputy in control of the 'military' side of the Munitions Department, i.e., that which is concerned with the actual design, manufacture and supply of the munitions of war." Lee called the 1915–1916 winter "the most critical period in the fortunes of the Allies." As of that date he judged that "we have survived remarkably well our miserable series of blunders and set-backs in the Balkans, Dardanelles, Mesopotamia and elsewhere"; nor could he detect "any serious crisis in the rambling structure of the Grand Alliance." Severe months of

---

[59] Strachey to Roosevelt, Oct. 26, 1915, *ibid.*
[60] Bryce to Roosevelt, Nov. 19, 1915, Roosevelt Papers.
[61] Spring Rice to Roosevelt, Nov. 19, 1915, Spring Rice Papers.

[62] Spring Rice to Roosevelt, Nov. 22, 1915, *ibid.*
[63] Roosevelt to Spring Rice, Nov. 24, 1915, Gwynn, 1929: 2: p. 288.
[64] *Ibid.,* p. 289.
[65] Spring Rice, Nov. 25, 1915, Spring Rice Papers.
[66] Spring Rice to Roosevelt, Nov. 30, 1915, *ibid.*

trial were ahead, nevertheless. "The real problem for the Alliance now," Lee told Roosevelt, "is to beat the enemy in what has really become a feverish race against time . . . this applies specially to the production of munitions. And here our chief difficulty is not with regard to money, machinery, or material, but with labour." As Lee explained, many of the most skilled men had enthusiastically enlisted in the services, while many with lesser skill had remained "oblivious to the call of patriotism." He indicated that he was not unsympathetic to the Trades Union fear that many of the labor gains could be lost due to wartime exigencies, but held that without some relaxation of the rules "we can not possibly complete our tasks in time." In so far as America and the war were concerned Lee was also apprehensive.

> Just at the moment there is a recrudescence of anxiety here about the attitude of the United States, and whilst I do not take the rumors in the Press very seriously I am not surprised that some people here are a good deal perturbed by Springey's [is he ill, by chance?] constant stream of despondent and almost alarmist dispatches. He seems to think the German element is becoming increasingly powerful in Congress, and that there is a real risk of some kind of embargo on the export of munitions to the Allies. . . . I may of course be entirely wrong but I cannot believe that talk of this description is going to materialize into any really dangerous action. Wilson does not inspire one with any special confidence in this or any connection, but I cannot believe that even he would be foolish enough to play for the German vote to the extent of sanctioning any kind of embargo.

Whereupon Lee asked to have Roosevelt's "analysis of the situation as it exists, *and your advice as to how we ought to proceed.* This would really be a great service, as I am now in a better position than I have been for a long time past to help in keeping things straight." Lee's letter concluded with a personal remark: would Roosevelt seek the presidency in 1916?

> I know of course that you have no political ambitions or any desire to run for the Presidency, but it seems more than likely that you may have to do it, not for your own sake but as the only means of preserving your country's honour and dignity in the world. . . . As I have often said, the English-speaking communities above all things prize a *man* who is not afraid to lead.[67]

Roosevelt's reply, sent off in haste just prior to sailing on a West Indian cruise, offered the advice which had been sought. The erstwhile chief of state kept the importance of the Anglo-American special relationship uppermost in what he had to say.

> . . . My judgment would be that it would be well for your people to make any unimportant concessions they can and do it with a great flourish of trumpets, but not to yield on anything that is vital. I have written Grey that, in my judgment, it is a great mistake not to give the American

people an idea of what the British have accomplished, especially in their submarine warfare.[68]

If, at this time, Roosevelt was considered by some of his English friends in any way as the head of a shadow government, then Great Britain could look forward to the 1916 presidential elections in the United States in hopes that so dedicated a friend might be once again chosen to lead the American people.

Letters passing between Roosevelt and Arthur Lee during these troubled months were not frequent, but when they did come they were marked by a spirit of abiding friendship. "Even on the very rare occasions when I am able to extricate a few minutes in the day from the ceaseless grind of work, I feel no inclination to see anyone or do anything, still less to write," Lee confided to his old friend in a letter of May, 1916. "And yet at these times I think perhaps more often of you and what you are doing than of anything else and become quite unreasonably impatient for direct news and letters which I have certainly done nothing to earn." The large affairs of state rather than his personal adjustment to the war preoccupied Lee and it was of these matters that he was anxious to give and have news of Roosevelt. For example, he intimated that he had lost confidence in Asquith's Coalition Government and wondered aloud to Roosevelt "as to whether it is my duty to leave it and go into active opposition. . . ." To Lee the Allies were clearly not winning, and a stalemate, as dramatized by Verdum, could bring about a disastrous peace. "During the past few weeks," he acknowledged to Roosevelt,

> there has been a sinister recrudescence of 'Peace' talk which is of course put about by the Germans who naturally would be delighted to sell out at the top of the market. These feelers often have an insidious effect upon weak and irresolute minds, but their danger lies mainly in the purely selfish use that is made of them by opportunist and cold blooded politicians like the Pope and President Wilson.

Despite the peace rumors, "the main thing that matters," Lee believed, "is to accumulate munitions and men." He applauded the fact that at least all-round conscription had been adopted which, in his view, had been "hailed with a sigh of relief by the public at large." Optimistic as he tried to be, Lee had to confess to his friend that

> we shall never *win* the war with this Government and largely because Asquith shares to a remarkable degree the very qualities which have endeared President Wilson to you and other red-blooded Americans. The strength of this brand of statesmanship lies in the fact that they have not the inclination or resolution to wage war to the bitter end and that almost any kind of plausible peace would be hailed at first with relief by a tired and short-sighted section of the public. As I have said already, if Peace comes this year it can only come as a disaster to the Allied cause.

---

[67] Lee to Roosevelt, Jan 26, 1916, Lee Papers. (Italics in original.)

[68] Roosevelt to Lee, Feb. 18, 1916, *ibid.*

Lee was also worried about a peace of exhaustion for Wilson then might step in to act as a mediator. But to him as to Roosevelt there was nothing to mediate: Germany was morally wrong and must be beaten. Such thinking could only lead Lee to hope that somehow Roosevelt would be elected president in 1916. Far removed from the realities of American politics and his judgments perverted by the pressures of war, surely his wish was father to his thought. He predicted to TR: "That you will be nominated and selected—unless conditions radically change before the next month—I firmly believe. . . . It seems almost inconceivable that the American people should be effectively fooled by the kind of politics that Wilson is playing at the moment." "You will perhaps remember," he went on, "that I always wanted to 'save you up' for 1916, and I am beginning to put this down to one of those queer presentiments which have come to me at various times (notably in connection with you) and which in my case perhaps form a substitute for deliberate judgment." Only occasionally during the course of the Roosevelt-Lee friendship did the strength of personal tie blind one or the other to the realities of a situation. But as Lee said to TR, "the war is getting a bit on my nerves" and under the impact of the frightful conflict Roosevelt's appeal as a *deus ex machina* was beguiling.[69]

Roosevelt replied to Lee on July 7, the day the Republican Convention met in Chicago. His tone was sober and remorseless. "No wonder your nerves are a little ragged from overwork and anxiety. I have to keep an iron hand on myself over here. . . ." "What you say about the military situation I, of course, agree . . ., at the present the Germans are on the whole victorious. . . ." "As you say, rash and irresolute minds among the Allies may be influenced by the cold blooded opportunism of men like the Pope and President Wilson." "I do not believe the Republicans have any intention of nominating me." "Our industrial unpreparedness is as great as our military unpreparedness." And finally Roosevelt closed this litany of lament: "May all good attend you and your country, my dear Arthur." [70]

Lee's answer to TR and to the decision of the Republican Convention, dated July 26, 1916, completed this series of letters. He described himself as completely dumbfounded by the nomination of Charles Evans Hughes, calling it a "great and unexpected shock." "I still believe of course—and I am confirmed in this view by almost every American whom I meet or hear from— that there was an overwhelming support for you amongst the rank and file of the Republican party and that if you had been nominated you would simply have romped in November." Lee spoke of the outcome as "nothing short of an international tragedy," because Roosevelt had been "deprived of an opportunity to act

as the arbitrator of peace." Fundamentally he feared the Allies could expect nothing by way of aid or encouragement from either Wilson, who was without "the slightest respect in Europe," or Hughes, whose "international reputation is at the present exactly nothing." The prospects of some sort of Anglo-American action were simply not now in the offing. The presence of Lloyd George at the head of the British government was the only bright spot, Lee maintained. Having worked under him at the Ministry of Munitions, Lee had concluded that Lloyd George was the one man who had sufficient decision and determination to push the war to the victory which was needed. In short, this was the kind of man that Roosevelt himself admired, according to Lee. TR asked his friend to convey his admiration to Lloyd George, which Lee did. In this small and informed way the driving personality behind the British government derived some sense of an Anglo-American commitment to the imperative of total victory at a time when the American government was perched on the fence.[71]

The nomination of Hughes by the Republicans in July and the victory of Wilson at the polls in November of 1916 profoundly disturbed Theodore Roosevelt and those of his English friends who held that Roosevelt's brand of leadership was essential to American participation in the war for Allied victory. St. Loe Strachey summed up these thoughts, when he wrote TR shortly after the election.

I, like I expect all your friends in this country, have felt very sad during the last few weeks at the thought of your disappointment over the election. It must, I know, have cut you to the heart to see your country, through a misunderstanding and clouding of the people's mind, led to endorse President Wilson's action; for it must be very difficult for any American who feels as you do to regard the election in any other light. I confess that personally I was deeply chagrined by the result. I am perfectly sincere when I say that my disappointment was not as an Englishman, but as a friend of America. I fully realize that America cannot help the Allies, and therefore, as far as we and the struggle are concerned, it does not matter to us in the very least whether it is Hughes or Wilson. The circumstances of the case now make it certain that America must continue the course she has adopted from the beginning. It is solely out of my respect and affection for America that I have been so deeply pained by Wilson's election.[72]

Similar postmortems of the 1916 election in the letters of TR and his friends, especially those of Strachey and Arthur Lee, underscored the fact that the British government had to deal with President Wilson and to shape its policies accordingly. Its course of action was to eschew the more advanced pro-British, pro-Allied Roosevelt position because it was clear the ex-president represented a minority American view. The people of

[69] Lee to Roosevelt, May 10, 1916, Roosevelt Papers; see also Lee to Roosevelt, June 7, 1916, Lee Papers.

[70] Roosevelt to Lee, July 7, 1916, Roosevelt Papers.

[71] Lee to Roosevelt, May 10, 1916, Roosevelt Papers; Roosevelt to Lee, July 7, 1916, *ibid.*; Lee to Roosevelt, July 26, 1916, *ibid.*

[72] Strachey to Roosevelt, Nov. 20, 1916, *ibid.*

the United States and their government had not as yet become convinced that their national interest was essentially tied to a British and Allied victory. All of this was poignantly evident in a letter Roosevelt sent Strachey about mid-summer, 1916, after the decision of the Republican convention. In the former president's judgment he was "fighting the battles of the Allies," for which Belgium was "pathetically grateful" and France showed "much appreciation." In England, however, ". . . Mr. Wilson seemed to have fooled the people" into thinking that he was pro-British. "I can entirely understand why from motives of policy the English has refrained from attacking Wilson; but to support him and strengthen him against men who have really stood for the Allies and for humanity . . . is a different thing." As this letter went on it revealed an even deeper source of frustration than a lack of political power, for Roosevelt admitted that a "considerable majority of my own countrymen" preferred Wilson's policy of watchful waiting to his own insistent demands for military involvement.[73] Strachey's response to Roosevelt's distress was a mixture of phantasy and politics.

I don't wonder you speak of the "curious features" in your experience of the last two years, namely the lack of support you have had in this country [England]. . . . Quite between ourselves (for I suppose this would be deemed a very disloyal thing for me to say, and I would not say it to anybody but you) it is the English government Wilson has fooled more than the English people. The idea has been that Wilson represents the attitude of the whole American people, and if we want to remain friends with America (as we all do) we must not dare say that he does not represent anything of the kind.

Phantasy overmastered Strachey as he continued.

Curiously enough, what you say as to what your policy would have been (and which I am sure it would have been) coincides with what I have always sketched in my own mind as to the ideal policy for the United States; not a policy of war—far from it—but a policy of insisting that the fight shall be conducted under the proper rules, and the nations should fight like gentlemen and not like wild boars. That sounds like sport, but is humanity. If the Germans had known the United States would take that attitude, they would never have dared, as you state, to brutalize Belgium or generally behave as they have behaved.[74]

All this was in keeping with Strachey's highly sentimental outlook on Anglo-American affairs, an attitude TR consistently opposed. Thus Strachey wrote his friend that he was compelled to resort to the pages of the *Spectator* to speak out on the issues of the 1916 election in America.

In the case of a nation like America about which I care a great deal I was going to claim the right of a friend and a blood relation and speak my mind quite frankly. I

would always take criticism of England from an American which I would never take from a foreigner because even if I am hurt and angry I admit that the blood relation has a right to speak the truth. With people we don't care about we smile and use polite words, which in effect mean, "By all means, my dear friend, go to the devil in your own way, it does not matter to me." That, please God is an attitude I will never take toward America.[75]

Given such emotions, the political events of 1916 in the United States could only be interpreted as a setback to Anglo-American welfare, both as to internal governmental stability and world dominion—the great objects of policy as envisioned by Roosevelt and his English correspondents.

Brooding over the election Strachey penetrated directly to the center of the pro-Wilson sympathy by the British government.

You, as having been one of the rulers of the world, know a great deal better than I do, what a curious freemasonry there is among governments. I have always been able to see here a kind of curious, unconscious or I might say instinctive sympathy for Wilson and, a dislike of criticism of him because of his policies. Or to put it another way, governments are never really in much sympathy with oppositions. They are always a little inclined, again unconsciously, to criticize the attitudes of the opposition and say that these people may all be right but they do not understand or make any proper allowances for the difficulties of government. Therefore I was always rather suspect because I took a line of my own and was a frank anti-Wilsonite. Personally as a man who speaks the English language and has nothing but British blood in his veins— English and Scotch—I refuse absolutely to treat the American people, kindred in race and language, and what is more important, kindred in ideals, at I treat a purely foreign country. I claim my right to say what I think about American action, as long of course as I say it decently. I will never admit that it is of no concern of mine—and of course I yield the same right of criticism of things here to all Americans.

And then he added more election post-mortems.

If Hughes had taken the line that you took and had spoken out perfectly, boldly and clearly against the Germans and said that he did not want the vote of a single one of them—

[73] Roosevelt to Strachey, July 22, 1916, *Roosevelt Letters* 8: pp. 1091–1094, *passim;* Bryce had said as much; see Bryce to Roosevelt, April 22, 1916, Roosevelt Papers.

[74] Strachey to Roosevelt, Sept. 23, 1916, Strachey Papers.

[75] *Ibid.* Strachey wrote to much the same point in November. ". . . I may be too optimistic but I think Grey overdoes his talk about the United States not being popular here just now. I think though unanalytical as a people we analyze better than that. I should have put it that the U. S. *Government* is not popular here just now. It should go further and say that Wilson is very unpopular and not because anybody thinks him unfriendly to this country, but because they think he is a hedging old domine with no guts. In a word, he is unpopular for the very opposite reasons that you are popular, i.e., you are popular because you speak out, hit hard, have a mind of your own and black people's eyes when you feel like it. They like you, in fact, because you have plenty of 'you be damnedness' about you. They dislike Wilson because he does not appear to be able to say NO to a goose, much less to a Bernstorff or a Bethman-Hollweg.
Hughes from this distance looks like a mummy. But I have your word for it that he is not, and so if I were an American and had a vote I should vote for him." Strachey to Roosevelt, Nov. 7, 1916, Strachey Papers. See also Roosevelt to Strachey, Dec. 15, 1916, *ibid.*

in fact hit them so hard that they would not vote for him—I believe he would have done much better. However, as Cromwell said, if you remember, these may be carnal thoughts.[76]

Nor was Strachey unwilling to attack the English government in the name of a more militant Anglo-American front. "All you say about that rotten League to Enforce Peace is honey to me," he wrote privately at the end of 1916.

I am very fond of Edward Grey but he certainly behaved like a prize jackass in having anything to do with it. Unfortunately he is not a man who studies history and therefore does not appreciate an analogy such as the history of the Holy Alliance affords . . . which is only the League to Enforce Peace over again.[77]

Believing as they did, the 1917 prospects for Roosevelt and his friends of some kind of active Anglo-American policy to bring Germany to her knees were hardly viable. Yet within the year the United States would be fully committed to winning the war through massive military and industrial involvement. Events demonstrated that there was more than one path leading to the broad thoroughfare of Anglo-American alliance, but that such a path would not be trod until Germany appeared a direct menace to American interest and security.

Though he had no major role to play in the Anglo-American war effort of 1917–1918, Theodore Roosevelt's bit part, despite its limitations, further illustrated the character of Anglo-American friendship which the war itself was to enlarge. Arthur Lee and St. Loe Strachey each suggested Roosevelt pay a visit to wartime England. Lee and his chief, Lloyd George, had in mind for Roosevelt to write a series of articles on Britain at war for the American public. Roosevelt's letter, declining Lee's invitation, advanced reasons consonant with Anglo-American accord. "If I went abroad I would give you no advice of even the slightest worth," he told Lee. "I would expose myself to bitter mortifications—no matter how much one condemns one's own country, one cannot stand condemnation of it by promiscuous outsiders (*you* may say *anything* and I will say ditto to it!)."[78] Somewhat later, Strachey also tried to persuade the former chief executive to spend time in England. "Why don't you come over and pay a good visit to our troops in the field? I need hardly say how delighted they and the whole nation

would be to see you."[79] But Roosevelt declined that offer as well. He had a hankering for battle and the thought of seeing British troops in training on the Salisbury Plain was no doubt attractive. But, as he told Lee, he would come only at the command of American troops.[80]

The desire of some of Roosevelt's friends to have him in England in the Winter of 1916–1917 should be read against the fact that at that time the low point in Anglo-American official relations had been reached. People like Lee and Strachey were trying, unconsciously perhaps, to maintain what all along they had considered the most vital link in the chain of Anglo-American friendship, the image of Theodore Roosevelt, an American unafraid to speak out forcefully in favor of Britain and the Allies. In light of the need of the British government to avoid further deterioration in relations with the United States this kind of private pleading was perhaps incautious. Yet to these men Roosevelt appeared as their only hope. "At a crisis when the news from the United States which contrives to reach us is abstruse and enigmatic, everything said by you, or about you, stands out so firm and clear and full of meaning," George O. Trevelyan wrote TR in February, 1917.[81] These were not simply the sentiments of an old man enamoured of a younger hero, but the projected feelings of all Englishmen who awaited a vigorous statement of the American stake in the war which, by the date of Trevelyan's letter, was fraught with new questions arising from Germany's resumption of unrestricted submarine warfare. If it was German folly which once again "swallowed up Anglo-American discontent,"[82] no group of men were more thankful for it than Theodore Roosevelt and his English friends, now including once more one who it appeared had fallen by the wayside, James Bryce. The new turn in German grand strategy was proof, superfluous to the Roosevelt circle, of the longstanding need for all right-thinking men actively to oppose Germany. Fittingly, Bryce wrote to Roosevelt in March of 1917:

From what I can gather it is all but certain that within the next three weeks and probably before this reaches you there will be a state of war between the United States and Germany. . . . If America is to fight she will, we trust, fight "not only with hands but with hatchets also." (It was an ancient Greek saying.)[83]

Theodore Roosevelt very much wanted to fight with hatchets. His reply to Bryce bore that mark, and another trait as well: continued skepticism concerning Woodrow Wilson as a wartime leader.

---

[76] Strachey to Roosevelt, Nov. 24, 1916, Strachey Papers.

[77] Strachey to Roosevelt, Dec. 30, 1916, Roosevelt Papers. Nor would Roosevelt give any quarter to Wilson. "What you have said about the peace proposals is capital. Wilson has played an evil part by his action; he is trying to bring about a peace as wicked as the peace which Prussia, France and a minority of the English leaders tried to induce Lincoln to accept." Roosevelt to Strachey, Jan. 1, 1917, *Roosevelt Letters* 8: p. 1139.

[78] Roosevelt to Lee, Nov. 10, 1916, *ibid.*, p. 1125. (Italics in original.)

[79] Strachey to Roosevelt, Nov. 20, 1916, Roosevelt Papers.

[80] Roosevelt to Lee, Nov. 10, 1916, Lee Papers. Lee also urged Roosevelt to come to England and to the Front after the United States entered the war but the idea TR turned down for political and personal reasons. See Roosevelt to Lee, Feb. 21, 1918, *Roosevelt Letters* 8: pp. 1288–1291.

[81] Trevelyan to Roosevelt, Feb. 17, 1917, Roosevelt Papers.

[82] Allen, 1955: p. 684.

[83] Bryce to Roosevelt, March 21, 1917, Bryce Papers.

I have urged that every vessel we have, suitable for war against the submarine, be sent to wherever your Admiralty deems it best. I have urged that we do everything in our power to furnish you cargo ships for food. This I think the President will try to do. I have also urged an immediate expeditionary force to France, and have asked leave to raise a division for it. The President, however, is down at the bottom of his heart—a pacifist, and not a fighting man and he is much more ready to help with food and boats and loans than with troops. I think this is an ignoble and shameful thing for our people.[84]

The need for dynamic leadership still existed despite American presence in the war: had history not passed Roosevelt by?

In the martial fulfillment of the Anglo-American alliance two important considerations emerged from the letters of Roosevelt and his friends. The first was the need to win the war by a total defeat of Germany; the second, to construct a peace which would secure free government at home and world power abroad. Discussion of both these objectives was somewhat limited, however. The requirement of total victory was too obvious to merit argument, while for the momentous problems of peace too little time was vouchsafed Roosevelt to assess in conjunction with his friends the realities of a postwar world.

TR's own proposal to raise a division was dismissed by the War Department as both impractical and ill-advised. The scheme, doubtless containing seeds of personal ambition, should also be considered expressive of the Anglo-American esprit. As Roosevelt informed both Spring Rice and Bryce, he believed it incumbent on the administration to get American fighting forces to the front as soon as possible.[85] Bryce pinpointed the reason in one of his letters to the former president. "The moral effect of the appearance in the War Line of an American force would be immense not merely as showing the German people that their cause is hopeless but by emphasizing the fact that their detestable inhuman methods have arrayed against them the conscience of the world." [86]

Roosevelt was able to join in the fighting only vicariously through his sons, all of whom entered military service. His youngest, Quentin, who was later killed in action, sought first to enlist in the Royal Flying Corps. Roosevelt senior had been firm, however, in insisting that his son must remain an American citizen.[87] Another son, Kermit, was commissioned in the British Air Force and served in Mesopotamia. In securing the commission TR sought to enlist the help of Arthur Lee: "I ask that he be permitted to render service to your flag as well as to my own. Will you try to help me, old Friend?" But again Roosevelt did not want

Kermit to forswear his allegiance to the United States but "merely to swear that he will loyally serve your King and Government for the length of this War." [88] Roosevelt's other boys, Theodore and Archibald, and his son-in-law, Richard Derby, joined the American forces. Spring Rice wrote in July, 1917: "I need not tell you and Mrs. Roosevelt how completely our hearts are with you and your sons. Make the sacrifice of righteousness and trust in the Lord." [89] From the personal perspective of Roosevelt and his friends the Anglo-Americans had closed ranks to do battle. Even James Bryce caught the spirit. "I wish you were in the war in France for I know what your presence there would mean to your troops and how it would be welcomed by ours," he wrote the colonel in October, 1917.

I wish also that the American troops were along side ours instead of divided by a piece of the French front. Far more could be accomplished for the common cause by an onrush side by side making a big hole in the German lines. . . . [I] hope that your men and ours will get to know one another in a way helpful not only for the present but for the future also.

And Bryce went on to suggest: "if active operations continue in Palestine, there are political reasons which you can easily divine, why an American *corps d'armée* operating in Syria would have much to commend it." [90] Roosevelt's reply echoed these martial tones:

Thank Heaven America has come into the war. I am going to indulge in the boastfulness of saying that if Mr. Wilson had accepted my offer when I made it on February 2nd, last, I would have had at least two divisions doing their part in the great and splendid British drive that has just taken place, and we Americans would have had the proud honor of spending our blood in the joint effort of the joint armies. . . . I am interested in your saying that you wish American troops were along side yours. I heartily agree with your views that it would be far better if your army were put in with ours.[91]

But the ordeal of battle would take its toll and old friends and dear would be at hand of offer solace. Bryce wrote Roosevelt upon news that TR's sons had been injured. "We are greatly concerned to hear that your two sons have been wounded, but I trust that those lightly wounded have recovered and that this will be the case with Archie also. You have good reason to be proud of your boys, as you have of your country.

---

[84] Roosevelt to Bryce, April 17, 1917, *ibid.*

[85] Roosevelt to Spring Rice, April 16, 1917, *Roosevelt Letters* 8: pp. 1174–1175; Roosevelt to Bryce, April 19, 1917, Bryce Papers; Roosevelt to Bryce, Nov. 26, 1917, *ibid.*

[86] Bryce to Roosevelt, March 21, 1917, *ibid.*

[87] Roosevelt to Spring Rice, April 16, 1917, Spring Rice Papers.

[88] Roosevelt to Lee, June 18, 1917, *Roosevelt Letters* 8: p. 1202.

[89] Spring Rice to Roosevelt, July 15, 1917, Spring Rice Papers.

[90] Bryce to Roosevelt, Oct. 25, 1917, Bryce Papers. See also Bryce to Roosevelt, April 6, 1918: "How you must be wishing, those of you who foresaw that the United States could not avoid coming into the war, that your preparations had begun in 1915 when the *Lusitania* was sunk! What would it have meant to have had a million of American soliders now in the field in France! However, already the moral support is enormous and the material support will grow from week to week." Fisher, 1920: 2: p. 184.

[91] Roosevelt to Bryce, Nov. 26, 1917, Bryce Papers.

It is perfectly splendid to see the spirit which your people are throwing into their efforts. Here in Europe very few understand what it means to Americans to have foregone the old traditional ideas of complete abstinence from Old World affairs, and what a moral passion must have swept over your country to make it throw itself in this struggle with such enthusiasm and energy. All that I hear from the front shows that they are fighting splendidly. . . ." [92] When Quentin was killed Roosevelt wrote to Arthur Lee: "There is nothing to be said about Quentin. It is very dreadful that he should have been killed; it would have been far worse if he had not gone." [93] The cause, and in great measure it was an Anglo-American cause, was worth the sacrifice.

When the war was over and won the problems of peace would be hard by. Roosevelt and his English friends agreed that peace was possible only by a total defeat of the German enemy. "Our greatest danger now," TR observed to Lee in August, 1917, "is the effort for 'peace without victory,' for which the Hearst and German papers and all the pro-Germans and pacifists now stand." Wilson, of course, was the nemesis of total victory. "His [Wilson's] antagonisms to Wood and myself," he added in his letter to Lee, "is partly because he has been obliged to reverse himself and come to the policy we have for three years advocated and partly because he feared we might get credit if we went to war." [94] Bryce observed to Roosevelt in the autumn of 1917: "*Now* what is needed is to exert every effort to shorten the war by convincing the German Government that it must be ultimately defeated." [95] In the name of complete German prostration TR told Lee: "Slowly but I believe surely, our people are waking, slowly they are growing to understand what the German horror is, and what it means." [96] Somewhat later Bryce made his point again. "I am delighted to see that you have been insisting so strongly and so firmly upon the necessity of a complete overthrow of the power of the German Government for evil. Nothing less will do. It must be so thoroughly discredited in the eyes of the German people as to be put out of commission for ever and ever." [97] In light of these sentiments Wilson's Fourteen Points looked exactly like the prelude to a negotiated peace. "The Fourteen Points were thoroughly mischievous and would have meant a negotiated peace with Germany," Roosevelt insisted to Arthur Lee in November, 1918, after Wilson had suffered his political setback in the off-year congressional elections. The former chief executive was convinced that the outcome of the elections was due to the desire of most Americans for total victory. The people, he told Lee, "wished unconditional surrender, and there was an outburst of popular feeling such as I have rarely seen in America. The president was repudiated and threatened by the people who had been his slavish adherents." [98] As prejudiced as this interpretation may have been, Roosevelt's own political star had started to take on a renewed luster. He had led the fight against Wilson on the broad issues of war and peace and he, or at least the Republican party, had triumphed in Wilson's defeat. Whatever the consequences of Roosevelt's election to the presidency in 1920, had that by chance occurred, the prospects that he would be nominated and elected had to be assessed seriously on both sides of the Atlantic after November, 1918.

In March, 1918, at Portland, Maine, in a speech widely reported in the press and in party circles. Theodore Roosevelt restated and in some ways enlarged on his Progressive beliefs of the 1912 canvass. This was a speech in which the possibility of the presidency itself could not have been entirely absent from the speaker's thoughts. Roosevelt called for tight federal regulation of the corporations but not at the expense of the right of labor to enjoy a larger share in the profits of business. He saw in these proposals the best way of avoiding class warfare in the United States. Public housing, assistance to agriculture, and various social security measures were also among his proposals. "Your Maine address is most interesting," Bryce commented in a letter. "All you say about the need for the melting pot to melt, and the efforts to be made for the economic reconstruction and better feeling between classes after the war is most true and reasonable." [99] Regarding his vision of a postwar era Roosevelt wrote to Lee about this time: "I am immensely struck by your speech to your constituents. It is so essentially like my speech to the Republican Convention in Maine that I sent you a copy of the latter. Our views of war and peace, of future international policy and of future internal policy, are curiously alike." [100] Roosevelt, reasserting the old Progressive ideas at home and demanding total victory abroad, appeared a highly dangerous opponent for the Wilson administration, even though in an actual gathering of votes for the presidency his domestic and his foreign policy, appealing as they did to hostile sections within the Republican party and the nation, might well cancel each other out. Progressives at home were frequently advocates of peace without victory in the war. Despite the fantasy of Roosevelt elected president in 1920—both hindsight and his death in 1919 tend to blur the image—his vision of the postwar world was one with which his English friends agreed, for they together had fostered such a world

---

[92] Bryce to Roosevelt, June 5, 1918, *ibid.*
[93] Roosevelt to Lee, Sept. 8, 1918, *Roosevelt Letters* 8: p. 1368.
[94] Roosevelt to Lee, Aug. 17, 1917, *ibid.*, 8: p. 1224.
[95] Bryce to Roosevelt, Oct. 25, 1917, Bryce Papers.
[96] Roosevelt to Lee, April 12, 1918, Lee Papers.
[97] Bryce to Roosevelt, Oct. 30, 1918, Bryce Papers.

[98] Roosevelt to Lee, Nov. 19, 1918, *Roosevelt Letters* 8: p. 1397.
[99] Bryce to Roosevelt, April 17, 1918, Bryce Papers.
[100] Roosevelt to Lee, March 25, 1918, *Roosevelt Letters* 8: 1303.

during the prewar years: stability at home and dominion overseas. In October, 1917, Bryce wrote to Roosevelt of his concern about internal political developments after the war.

Here in Europe, both in France and Britain, great political changes are expected to follow the war. Socialism in France, "Labourism," which is mostly Socialism in England, have gained such strength as to give them a possible majority in each legislature if not immediately, yet very soon. At the same moment we have the spectacle of the hideous breakdown of an attempted democracy in Russia. . . . I gather that in the United States labour troubles are feared after the war. Otherwise your sky seems less cloudy than that of Europe.[101]

Roosevelt responded with an emphatic support of the established ways of politics.

I can not help hoping and believing England, France and America, with the Russian example before them, will show some reluctance to try any experiment that will tend to produce anarchy. . . . Here in the United States what is needed is resolute leadership to secure justice for the laboring man and the farmer and this we can not have without vision; but we also need equally resolute insistance that there should be no disorder and none of the cracked-brain action, which under the pretense of lifting the lowly, merely smashes the man on top and brings down everybody under its ruins.[102]

The internal strength of the victorious Powers would of course help to guarantee a world order in which the Anglo-Americans had a leading role to play.

To James Bryce the world order of the new era was of the utmost importance. He had faith that some kind of world body would be constructed that could guarantee international peace, and he was aware of Roosevelt's doubts about the proposed League of Nations. "I wish you would indicate what you think can be done to avert the recurrence of of such another calamity." he asked Roosevelt. "Britain, France and Italy can't go on supporting gigantic armaments; we are almost beggared already. Something must be done for common safety." [103] TR's views were contained in a letter to Bryce written some months later.

I absolutely agree with a lot you say about peace. I do not myself think there will be need of so much wisdom as firmness in settling the terms of peace. The principles are in outline simple enough. I have been preaching them here! England and Japan must keep the colonies they have won. France receive back Alsace-Lorraine, Belgium be restored and indemnified. Italia irredenta must go to Italy, down to Istria. The Czecho-Slovak, Polish and Jugo-Slav commonwealths must be created entirely independent; the latter with access to the Adriatic. Albania should be a cantonal state under the protection of France, England and perhaps the United States; the Turk should be driven from Europe. Armenia should be independent under a guarantee of the Allies; the Jews given Palestine, the Syrian Christians protected; the Arabs made independent. The separate nationalities of broken-up Russia should

be made commonwealths absolutely free from German dominion and probably independent; the Poles, the Slavs of Siberia, and the Danes of North Schleswig should all be free from the German yoke.[104]

The stamp of Anglo-American responsibility for world order in the foregoing projections was unmistakable. Roosevelt wrote much the same thing to Arthur Lee a month later.

I have been devoting some of my attention to public insistence that the British must keep the colonies they have taken from Germany. It would be a crime not to do so; and to propose to have the natives settle the matter by vote would be worthy of Bedlam were it not so transparently dishonest. I wish that good Edward Grey would not continue to blast with feeble amiability about securing universal peace through a League of Nations. It exactly corresponds to the peace talk of the anti-Lincoln men in 1864. It distracts attention from the prime duty of winning the war, and plays right into the hands of the pro-Germans and pacifists who are only waiting the chance to clamor that the slaughter must stop, that no nation must be punished, and all future war prevented by a League—of which Germany, Austria, Turkey and Russia would be four guarantors![105]

For all his advocacy of a League animated by a spirit of justice, Bryce's own formula, as he gave it to Roosevelt, suggested that justice was to be meted out and maintained especially by the Anglo-Americans. Thus he wrote to his American friend in October, 1918.

I am publishing a small volume of Essays, in one of which you will see a brief summary of the various questions relating to Nationalities, which have to be dealt with. Among those the most difficult seems to be that of Poland where the nation is, as it always was, greatly divided, and that of the Western parts of what was the Russian Empire. On the whole the best plan seems to be to make Finland completely independent, to allow the Finns, the Esthonians, the Letts, and the Lithuanians to choose and determine their own fates. Probably they would be stronger if they agreed to federate. The Ukraine is more difficult. I rather doubt whether the bulk of the people wish to be separated from Great Russia, and though we might wish that no power so large as the old Great Russia was before 1917 should hereafter arise, still we are not entitled to disregard the wishes of the Ukrainians, Little Russians and Ruthenians, by which ever name you call them. As respects Asia, the thing that must be absolutely and finally done, as I believe you have already stated, is to get rid of the Unspeakable Turk. Let him never again have the power to massacre Christians. I earnestly hope that the voice of America will speak out very clearly upon this subject. Nowhere have the Armenians and Syrians received warmer sympathy, nowhere so much charitable help, as in the U.S.A., and your people will surely make it clear that these populations should be completely liberated from the Turk. Enver and Talaat, the two chief villains, ought to be hanged if they can be caught. There is the story that Enver has escaped to the Caucasus, and is trying to make himself head of a kind of Principality there. It is of the greatest importance to be sure that the wills of the peoples are plainly expressed in all these matters, because I am

---

[101] Bryce to Roosevelt, Oct. 25, 1917, Bryce Papers.
[102] Roosevelt to Bryce, Nov. 26, 1917, *ibid.*
[103] Bryce to Roosevelt, April 17, 1918, *ibid.*
[104] Roosevelt to Bryce, Aug. 7, 1918, *ibid.*
[105] Roosevelt to Lee, Sept. 8, 1918, *Roosevelt Letters* **8**: pp. 1368–1369.

sure the peoples, yours and ours, and doubtless the French and Italians also, though they are much less instructed, will desire that Freedom and Nationality should be vindicated; and at all diplomatic conferences heretofore there has been a dangerous tendency to huddle things up by compromises. Never were there so many difficulties to be solved as now.[106]

If England and America were able to dominate the League and the other arrangements of the peace, Anglo-American hegemony, in a new form, would be sustained. Responding to Bryce's views, Roosevelt had a word of advice to offer that suggested once again the solidarity between the Allies and the people of America. "At the Peace Conference England and France can get what they wish, so far as America is concerned, if, while treating Wilson with politeness, they openly and frankly throw themselves on the American people for support in any vital matter." [107]

Yet these were no more than scraps of commentary on the postwar world. The shadows had begun to lengthen on Roosevelt and his English friends. Bryce intimated this in a letter to TR in which he had discussed the general trend of future politics in England and America. "Indeed America is the only country in which political conditions seem to have slowly but steadily improved during the last fifty years—a comforting thought for those of us who feel that their time for observing the ebbs and flows of human society is drawing to a close." [108] Spring Rice died in February, 1918, on his way home from his ambassadorial post, "just when an evening of peace seemed to be before him after the sultry day of his time in Washington." [109] Theodore Roosevelt himself would be dead before the Peace Conference was underway. With his death in January, 1919, the latch-pin of friendship had fallen free. Yet the alliance which those friendships had helped to father endured because of the foundations upon which it had been built, a singular combination of mutual esteem and determined self-interest. Roosevelt who did so much to foster Anglo-American accord must be allowed to have the last words. From the hospital on November 19, 1918, he wrote letters to both James Bryce and Arthur Lee. He and Bryce had had frequent talks in the past about the possibility of some kind of formal intergovernmental organization which would be invested with the power to adjudicate disputes between the American and the British governments.

Roosevelt now restated his attitude with the greatest of emphasis.

I hate not to face facts. It is a fact that the British Empire and the United States have reached the point, where, in my judgment, they can agree henceforth to arbitrate everything without reservation. I should be perfectly willing to establish a permanent Supreme Court, which would arbitrate any questions between these two nations (or any constituent portions of them) precisely as our own Supreme Court arbitrates questions affecting the different states. But I would not for one moment make any such arrangements as regards Germany, Russia, China, and most of the tropical American states—the reasons being different in different cases.[110]

To TR the mutual esteem of the English and American peoples was that real. But on the same day he wrote to Arthur Lee in a manner suggesting that singular self-interest could not be absent from the partnership.

As regards England, I end the war more convinced than ever that there should be the closest alliance between the British Empire and the United States; and also I am more convinced than ever that neither one can afford for one moment to rely on the other in a sufficiently tight place. There would always of course be the chance that the other, in such event, would wake up to the needs of the situation; but there would also be the chance that its own political tricksters and doctrinaires and sentimental charlatans and base materialists would make it false to its duty.[111]

We are led, at the last, to ponder Roosevelt's thoughts. The importance of national self-interest, as that was judged by the respective governments and by the Roosevelt circle of friends, was a consistent feature of the Anglo-American entente from its inception in 1898 through the testing of its strength in the fires of the 1914 war. And so it would be in the interwar period until, in Churchill's phrase, "the New World stepped forth to the rescue and liberation of the Old." National self-interest, however, need not be divisive. If the fundamental values of the two peoples are alike, if their histories have much in common, if their institutions enjoy a nurturing relationship, if their peoples see much to admire in each other while not yielding criticism to friendship, then the national self-interest, in time of crisis no less than in time of calm, can become a mutual self-interest. In the world of the twentieth century only the Anglo-Americans, not the least of whom were Theodore Roosevelt and his English friends, have known and profited from such accord.

---

[106] Bryce to Roosevelt, Oct. 30, 1918, Bryce Papers.

[107] Roosevelt to Bryce, Nov. 19, 1918, *Roosevelt Letters* **8**: pp. 1399–1400; 1400.

[108] Bryce to Roosevelt, Oct. 25, 1917, Bryce Papers.

[109] Bryce to Roosevelt, April 17, 1918, *ibid.*

[110] Roosevelt to Bryce, Nov. 19, 1918, *Roosevelt Letters* **8**: p. 1400.

[111] Roosevelt to Lee, Nov. 19, 1918, *ibid.*, **8**: p. 1398.

BIBLIOGRAPHY

PRIMARY SOURCES

James Bryce Papers, Bodleian Library, Oxford
Arthur H. Lee Papers, Private
Theodore Roosevelt Papers, Library of Congress
Cecil Spring Rice Papers, Private
St. Loe Strachey Papers, Private

SECONDARY WORKS

ALLEN, H. C. 1955. *Great Britain and the United States* (New York).

BEALE, HOWARD K. 1956. *Theodore Roosevelt and the Rise of America to World Power* (Baltimore).

BISHOP, JOSEPH B. 1920. *Theodore Roosevelt and his Times* (2 v., New York).

BLAKE, NELSON. "Ambassadors at the Court of Theodore Roosevelt." *Miss. Valley Hist. Rev.* 42 : pp. 179–206.

BRYCE, JAMES. 1897. *The American Commonwealth* (2 v., New York).

BURTON, DAVID H. 1968. *Theodore Roosevelt Confident Imperialist* (Philadelphia).

CAMPBELL, A. E. 1960. *Great Britain and the United States, 1895–1903* (London).

CAMPBELL, C. S. 1957. *Anglo-American Understanding, 1898–1903* (Baltimore).

ESTHUS, RAYMOND A. 1967. *Theodore Roosevelt and Japan* (Seattle and London).

FISHER, H. A. L. 1920. *James Bryce* (2 v., London).

GELBER, L. M. 1938. *The Rise of Anglo-American Friendship* (New York).

GRENVILLE, J. A. S. 1964. *Lord Salisbury and Foreign Policy* (London).

GWYNN, STEPHEN. 1929. *The Letters and Friendships of Sir Cecil Spring Rice* (2 v., Cambridge, England).

NEALE, R. G. 1966. *Great Britain and United States Expansion 1898–1900* (East Lansing).

NEARY, PETER. 1965. The Bryce Embassy to the United States 1907–1913." London University, unpublished Ph.D. dissertation.

NEU, CHARLES E. 1967. *An Uncertain Friendship Theodore Roosevelt and Japan* (Cambridge, Massachusetts).

NISH, IAN. 1966. *The Anglo-Japanese Alliance* (London).

PERKINS, BRADFORD. 1968 . *The Great Rapprochement, England and the United States 1895–1914* (New York).

RANSOM, E., "British Military and Naval Observers in the Spanish-American War." *Jour. Amer. Studies* 3 : pp. 33–56.

ROOSEVELT, THEODORE. 1913. *An Autobiography* (New York). 1922–1926. *The Works of Theodore Roosevelt* (24 v., New York). Herein cited as *Works*.

——. 1951–1954. *The Letters of Theodore Roosevelt,* ed. by Elting E. Morison (8, v., Cambridge, Massachusetts). Herein cited as *Roosevelt Letters*.

RUSSETT, BRUCE M. 1963. *Community and Contention Britain and America in the Twentieth Century* (Cambridge, Massachusetts).

SEED, GEOFFREY. 1958. "British Reactions to American Imperialism Reflected in Journals of Opinion, 1898–1900." *"Pol. Sci. Quart.* 73 : pp. 254–272.

STRACHEY, AMY. 1930. *St. Loe Strachey His Life and Letters* (London).

STRACHEY, ST. LOE. 1922. *The Adventure of Living* (London).

WATT, D. C. 1963. "American and British Foreign Policy-Making Elites, From Joseph Chamberlain to Anthony Eden, 1895–1956." *Review of Politics* 25 : pp. 3–33.

INDEX

MEMOIRS

OF THE

AMERICAN PHILOSOPHICAL SOCIETY

Aftermath of War: Bainbridge Colby and Wilsonian Diplomacy.   DANIEL M. SMITH.
Vol. 80.   x, 173 pp., 1970.   Paper. $2.00.

Census of the Exact Sciences in Sanskrit.   Series A, Volume I.   DAVID PINGREE.
Vol. 81.   viii, 60 pp., 1970.   Paper. $5.00.

Henry Wansey and His American Journal, 1794.   Edited by DAVID J. JEREMY.
Vol. 82.   xviii, 186 pp., 34 figs., 9 maps, 1970. $7.00.

The Inscriptions of Kourion.   T. B. MITFORD.
Vol. 83.   xvii, 422 pp., illus., 1971. $20.00.

Sir William Dawson: A Life in Science and Religion.   CHARLES F. O'BRIEN
Vol. 84.   x, 207 pp., 1971.   Paper. $3.00.

The Woolsey Sisters of New York: A Family's Involvement in the Civil War and a New Profession (1860-1900).
ANNE L. AUSTIN.
Vol. 85.   xviii, 189 pp., 19 figs., 1971.   Paper. $3.00.

Census of the Exact Sciences in Sanskrit.   Series A, Volume 2.   DAVID PINGREE.
Vol. 86.   viii, 147 pp., 1971.   Paper. $6.00.

The Swedish Bullionist Controversy: P. N. Christiernin's Lectures on the High Price of Foreign Exchange in
Sweden (1761).   ROBERT V. EAGLY.
Vol. 87.   x, 119 pp., 1971.   Paper. $2.00.

Darwin's Victorian Malady: Evidence for its Medically Induced Origin.   JOHN H. WINSLOW.
Vol. 88.   x, 94 pp., 1971.   Paper. $2.00.

Pāṇini's Metalanguage.   HARTMUT SCHARFE.
Vol. 89.   viii, 53 pp., 1971.   Paper. $5.00.

The Role of Providence in the Social Order.   JACOB VINER.   Jayne Lectures for 1966.
Vol. 90.   x, 113 pp., 1972. $2.00.

Les Seigneurs de Nesle en Picardie (12e Siècle à 1286).   WILLIAM M. NEWMAN.
Vol. 91.   2 pts., 787 pp., 1971. $25.00.

Gardening Ants, the Attines.   NEAL A. WEBER.
Vol. 92.   xviii, 146 pp., 192 figs., 1972. $8.00.

A Commentary on the Dresden Codex: A Maya Hieroglyphic Book.   J. ERIC S. THOMPSON.
Vol. 93.   x, 156 pp., 25 pls. (in color), 1972. $25.00.

New and Full Moons 1001 B. C. to A. D. 1651.   HERMAN H. GOLDSTINE.
Vol. 94.   viii, 221 pp., 1973. $5.00.

The Diary of Elihu Hubbard Smith (1771–1798).   Edited by JAMES E. CRONIN.
Vol. 95.   xvi, 481 pp., 1 fig., 1973. $15.00.

TRANSACTIONS

OF THE

AMERICAN PHILOSOPHICAL SOCIETY

TRANSACTIONS

OF THE

AMERICAN PHILOSOPHICAL SOCIETY

HELD AT PHILADELPHIA
FOR PROMOTING USEFUL KNOWLEDGE

NEW SERIES—VOLUME 63, PART 2
1973

THEODORE ROOSEVELT AND HIS ENGLISH CORRESPONDENTS: A SPECIAL RELATIONSHIP OF FRIENDS

DAVID H. BURTON
Department of History, St. Joseph's College, Philadelphia

THE AMERICAN PHILOSOPHICAL SOCIETY
INDEPENDENCE SQUARE
PHILADELPHIA

MARCH, 1973

DATE DI

PUBLICATIONS

OF

The American Philosophical Society

The publications of the American Philosophical Society consist of PRO-
CEEDINGS, TRANSACTIONS, MEMOIRS, and YEAR BOOK.

THE PROCEEDINGS contains papers which have been read before the Society in addition to other papers which have been accepted for publication by
the Committee on Publications. In accordance with the present policy one
volume is issued each year, consisting of six bimonthly numbers, and the
price is $5.00 net per volume.

THE TRANSACTIONS, the oldest scholarly journal in America, was started
in 1769 and is quarto size. In accordance with the present policy each annual volume is a collection of monographs, each issued as a part. The current
annual subscription price is $15.00 net per volume. Individual copies of the
TRANSACTIONS are offered for sale. This issue is priced at $3.00.

Each volume of the MEMOIRS is published as a book. The titles cover
the various fields of learning; most of the recent volumes have been historical.
The price of each volume is determind by its size and character.

The YEAR BOOK is of considerable interest to scholars because of the reports on grants for research and to libraries for this reason and because of the
section dealing with the acquisitions of the Library. In addition it contains
the Charter and Laws, and lists of present and former members, and reports
of committees and meetings. The YEAR BOOK is published about April 1 for
the preceding calendar year. The current price is $5.00.

An author desiring to submit a manuscript for publication should send it
to the Editor, George W. Corner, American Philosophical Society, 104 South
Fifth Street, Philadelphia, Pa. 19106.